Write the Book, Sis! An Interactive Guide to Writing A Powerful Book Your Audience Will Want to Read

Published by: The Literary Revolutionary, an Imprint of YBF Publishing, LLC.

www.theliteraryrevolutionary.com

Copyright © 2018 Nia Sadé Walker. (Nia Sadé Akinyemi) Without limiting the rights under copyright reserved above, no part of this publication may be reproduced, stored in or introduced into a retrieval system, or transmitted, in any form, or by any means (electronic, mechanical, photocopying, recording, or otherwise), without the prior written permission of both the copyright owner and the publisher of the book.

Manufactured in the United States of America

ISBN #: 978-0-9968910-5-9

Cover Design, Editing, & Formatting: YBF Publishing Team

Facebook.com/theliteraryrevolutionary

Instagram: @NiaSadeAkinyemi & @TheLiteraryRevolutionary

Twitter: @NiaSadeAkinyemi

www.theliteraryrevolutionary.com

Testimonials

If you ever wanted to write a book but didn't know where or how to start, this is who to talk to. This is my editor and sister, and she's awesome! She WILL make that book in your head real, if you let her.

– **Queen K** (Editing Client)
Author of Books "I Have Good Hair" & "My Beautiful Hair"

Nia was an integral factor to me becoming a first time author! I'm so grateful for and impressed with her passion, knowledge, flexibility, and resourcefulness as my literary coach. I can't say enough how helpful and relieving it was for me to be able to depend on her throughout this entire process. This coming from a recovering perfectionist, I believe means a little something. I would and have recommended her services to those I know.

–**Denesha Chambers** (Partner Publishing Client)
Author of "Turning Toward the Sun"

I have an emotional courage I would not have had without Nia's assistance. If you are merely flirting with the idea of having Nia help you with your book, do it. The guidance, expertise, and emotional support needed to birth your book; Nia can make that happen."

–**Anana Johari Harris Parris** (Partner Publishing Client)
Author of "Self Care Matters A Revolutionary's Approach"

Praise for #WriteTheBookSis!

Your book is definitely necessary for US, yes, us - the sisters, ready to write. -**Ke'Yonna H.**

I appreciate your wisdom more than you know! I live for this hashtag: #WriteTheBookSis!!! It's become a daily saying for me. Thank you sis for your guidance! -**Angelique N.**

Your information is inspiring, uplifting, and motivational to stir up desires to write a book! -**Willene W.S.**

I'm juggling a few things around trying to figure out how I'm going to make it work, but I'm going to take your advice and write the book, sis! Salute. –**M.D.**

I must say, you are a true gem! There's this undeniable fire that burns when I write, so this is the year of WRITE THE DAMN BOOK, SIS! –**Danielle N.**

You inspire me to WRITE MORE! – **Jasmine T.**

Also By Nia:

Young Black Fearless: The 7 Step Guide to Activism

Write for the Win

The Authorpreneur Agenda (Coming Next)

Write the Book, Sis!

Written By: Nia Sadé Akinyemi

Dedication

I dedicate *Write the Book, Sis!* to all the amazing women ancestors of color who wrote their hearts out and had to fight to publish their works; who endured the criticisms, the challenges, the doubt, and still… she wrote the book.

I THANK YOU.
I LOVE YOU.
I HONOR YOU.

You are the REAL Literary Revolutionaries.

With Love,
Nia Sadé Akinyemi

Acknowledgements

Thank you to all of my loved ones who pour into me daily and help me in ways that I can't even begin to explain. To my son, Israel, who is the very reason I go so hard about setting the example of what it means to truly be in control of your destiny. I pray every day that my decision to become a full-time Authorpreneur so that I can homeschool you is not in vain. I pray that you see me, you understand why, and you take notes for your own future. To my love, Carlos, I thank God for you. Your love, support, and unyielding display of teamwork and partnership make my days brighter. If I don't tell you enough, I truly appreciate you for everything you have contributed to my life, this brand, and our empire. I love you both from the bottom of my heart and I'm so grateful I get to do life with you two. May the blessings from this book shower down on not only our family, but the lives of each woman who reads and creates her best books from the instruction I deliver within these pages.

To the Sisterhood that is forming from this movement, I'm humbled by your existence and proud of the books that have been and will continue to be birthed along the journey. We are here and it is time. Write the Book, Sis!

Table of Contents

Acknowledgements	11
A Message from the Author	15
Introduction	17

Read As You Need:

If You're Wondering *IF* You Should Write A Book	21
When You Have No Clue Where to Start	29
When You Have Started Writing & Stopped	43
When You Begin to Get Discouraged	59
When Your Book is Almost Complete	65
When You Are Ready to Publish Your Book	87
When You Decide to Self-Publish Your Book	97
When Your Book Is Finally In Your Hands	111
Tips for Your Genre	115
-Nonfiction	117

-Fiction	119
-Memoirs/Autobiographies	125
-Children's Books	129
Does Your Brand Need A Book?	131
About the Author	145

A Message from the Author

This book is a tool you can use to help you manifest that powerful book you have inside of you. I have written it in a way where you can read what you need, as you need it. If you've ever attended any of my LIVE Series Sessions on Instagram, any of my Trainings, or Masterclasses, then you know I am all about participation. Getting you excited to join in on the conversation is my M.O. This book is set up no differently. There's no order to the pages you will turn; read it as you need it, sis.

I want you to use this book like most people use the Bible. Pick and choose what you need (or what you want to follow) at your own pace. There's absolutely no need to rush through the book, and by all means, please don't think you need to read it in its entirety if it doesn't apply to you. My goal is to help you turn that book idea into a finished manuscript ready to be flipped by a bomb editor (me) and either self-published by the gangsta author that is YOU, or partner-published with the gangsa publisher that is ME.

When you've taken the chance to read through and grab the tools you need, and once your book is completed, published, and in your hand – I want you to do me a favor, sis. I want you to let everyone and their grandmother know you wrote and published a powerful book that people need to read! You deserve everything good that comes from the birth of this book baby and I'm committing to helping you see it through.

Introduction

Major Key Alert – They don't want you to win, but I DO.

I don't know what your story is but I'd like to believe that because you are reading this book, you know you have a book of your own inside of you. I mean, **LET'S BE REAL...** You wouldn't be reading the first line in this book if you weren't thinking about writing one. Am I right? For that, I would like to say *congratulations* on identifying that you have something to say that can't be limited to just a Facebook post or a YouTube video. You have made the decision to at least see if writing this book you're thinking of is worth it. Maybe, you want to see if you have what it takes to pull it off, or maybe you've been charged to put your words, knowledge, or expertise into written form, so here you are.

Well, you have come to the right place, at the right time, and with the WRITE person. I am Nia Sade Akinyemi, best known as, *"The Literary Revolutionary"*. I teach people how to revolutionize their brands through writing, publishing, and marketing powerful books with ease and confidence. I help my clients flip their manuscripts into literary masterpieces through my author coaching, editing, and partner publishing services. People often come to me when they have a story to tell, a skillset to share, advice to give, or expertise to offer and they want to put it in a book. I pride myself in helping my clients gain respect as authorities in their lives and in their fields through writing and publishing books.

In this book, I am going to teach you how to turn what you know to be true into a masterpiece that no one will be able to deny, even if they disagree. Throughout this book you will learn WHY you have been called to document your words, HOW you're going to do it even when it may seem overwhelming, WHERE you're going to get your support from and the target audience who will buy it, WHEN you should release it, and WHAT you're doing it all for.

One of my favorite quotes comes from none other than DJ Khaled. It's the one where he says, "They don't want you to win." Thus, the reason for this major key. They (no matter who "they" may be to you) don't want to you win, but guess what? I DO! I want you to do the thing that excites you or scares you the most. I'll be the first to say, writing a book is not an easy thing to do. It takes time, discipline, proper preparation, research, resources, money and energy to get the job done. However, the job becomes so much easier when you have a positive support system pushing you along the way and you're working toward the goal not by yourself, but with a writing coach like me in your back pocket. I got you, sis!

Before you begin to feel like this may be too much, listen to me. YOU CAN DO THIS. I promise you! There's no better feeling than to finally share with the world your words through published text. Don't be afraid to step out on this journey. YOU'VE GOT THIS. Work on this book with the end in mind, but don't forget to enjoy the process. Before we get into the content, I want you to repeat this affirmation below:

"What I have to say is worth saying. What I have to write is worth writing. I will be glad when I have completed the process of writing and publishing MY book. It will all be worth it in the end."

Read This:
If You're Wondering *IF* You Should Write A Book

Becoming an author and having a book title under your list of achievements is a win on any level. A published book can do a lot, in what could seem as a small capacity. When I host *The Literary Revolutionary's Writing Workshop Experience* around the country, I always like to start with why one should write a book. Discussed below are my reasons and explanations as to why writing a book is and can be a phenomenal move to make.

<u>Writing a book makes you smart.</u>

Let's be honest. When someone identifies as an author, a certain level of esteem is given. This person is "smart", even if it's credited to merely having the gall to actually put their words into a printed book. We live in a society where perception is everything. People who write books are perceived as "smart" whether they are or not, whether their work is quality or crap. Taking the initiative to document whatever you believe is worth documenting is an intelligent move. At the end of the day, someone will need the words you put into a book and it's better to have one than not to have one.

One of my biggest fears is watching some of the most inspiring, educated, and wisdom-filled elders leave this earth without them having written a book. It's a sad situation because I can't help but to look at them as walking history books or motivational self-help books. What are we to do when they transition and their words, thoughts, knowledge, and wisdom goes to the grave with them? It's a major loss. It terrifies my soul and it's one of the very reasons I write and encourage others to do the same.

Writing a book can advance your career and/or business opportunities.

For those who are business minded and are planning to take a big step into your respective careers, a book can certify you as an expert in your field. I have literally witnessed someone who was extremely qualified for a job (even more qualified than their counterpart) lose to the person who had written a book. It can seem unfair in a sense, but the person who wrote the book made themselves stand out from the competition.

I come into contact with many people who ask me how I got started securing speaking engagements. They inquire how was it that people invited me to come sit on panel discussions, facilitate workshops, and get paid to speak to hundreds and thousands of people at a time. The answer is not at all simple, but let me put it into perspective for you.

Before my first book was written, I had to work extra hard to get speaking engagements. Even with all my efforts, I rarely got the opportunities I had hoped for on the first few attempts. The major key for me to begin getting into the doors and talking to the crowds of people I wanted to, was having a book to my name and always having it on hand. My daddy used to tell me that if I didn't go all the way through school, receiving not only my Bachelor's Degree, but my Masters and Doctorate degrees as well, it would be difficult for me to get asked to speak anywhere because those who were educated and had multiple degrees would always be asked first. Several years later, I can easily say that my Pops only offered one approach. Although he had a point, his analysis of how to make it happen wasn't the only way.

As soon as I had a book written, published, and in my hand, I no longer had to knock on doors and ask them to hear me out.

People who were looking for a speaker in the areas of interest that I had strong suits in were blowing my phone up trying to book me. My book became my ticket and I no longer had to hustle hard to get on the stages I was trying to reach. My book was my smart hustle. Those ten days of writing, revising, and organizing all of my written material was the small sacrifice I had to make to be in position to always be prepared when opportunities knocked on my door. My former mentor, Hotep, wrote in his book *"The Hustler's 10 Commandments"* that success comes when opportunity meets preparation. When he taught me this commandment, I put on my full time grind and did what I had to do to always be prepared when opportunities presented itself, which included writing my book.

Writing a book has therapeutic/healing qualities.

Nothing can help to release pain better than writing it out. I learned this through experience, as I remember always taking to pen and paper to express myself as a young teen. Journals and notebooks scattered across my bed and around my room growing up were a norm. It became such a release for me that when I was put on punishment as a child, my parents would take my journals and notebooks from me. I could not have the luxury of pouring all my thoughts onto paper. It was something I enjoyed so it was treated just like the television. They had to ensure that I would sit and think about why I was in trouble.

Writing about love, breakdowns, mental illnesses, trauma, disaster, neglect, harm, etc. is a way to make it to the next day. Writing can be (and oftentimes, is) a saving grace.

Writing a book can create another source of income.

Some people who write books are driven by the possibilities of their books reaching hundreds and thousands of people. These people have dreams of their words resonating with any and every one, with hopes that their book will make them famous. There are other authors that simply want to get paid, and there's absolutely nothing wrong with that. Writing a book can create that extra source of income that you may or may not have been hoping for. Just like any product, you have to be prepared to sell your merchandise. In this case, if you market yourself appropriately as it pertains to your message, your industry or your genre, you will have no problem making money.

Everyone is not able to get their book in stores around the world. As a matter of fact, if you don't have plans to shop your manuscript around to several major publishing companies that already have relationships in place for distribution, you will more than likely be making these strides as an independent author.

    The great thing about doing it on your own is making sure the integrity of your work is maintained and that you have all rights to how your work is used, and where it goes at all times. People who sign to major publishing companies can't always say the same. When you don't have to worry about publishing companies ripping you off and taking close to or more than half of your royalties, you are much better off.

    Imagine that. If your book is somewhere in between 100-200 pages of material, you can run that book anywhere from $9.99-$19.99 if you wanted. If you sell 50 books on your own for $9.99, that's an easy $500.00. If you sell 100 books on your own for $19.99, that is a smooth $2,000.00. Writing a book (or several books for that matter) can be an easy side hustle if you've got the talent and the hustle to sell them.

Writing a book allows your words to live forever.

    There are quite a few reasons you might consider writing a book. It could be that you have always had the desire to write a book or you've dreamed of becoming a published author. For some people, the notoriety of being labeled an author isn't as important as simply expressing their art through written form. For others, the author title is an added plus to the many other powerful things they are working to accomplish. Whether you choose to write for leisure or for career advancement, always keep in mind that your choice to write a book is a great one. If it does nothing else it is a piece of you that will live on for eternity once you transition to the other realm. It is a piece of you that will be left behind for future generations to read and study from. You will live forever and that can be one of the most precious gifts you give to the world.

Why You Should Listen to Me

I'll give you four reasons why you should listen to me, because I get it. You don't know me from a grain of salt if you haven't been following me for a while. I will be the first to admit that I don't always believe "the hype" of people that claim to be authorities in a given field either. It takes a lot to trust those who claim to know the knowledge you seek, so let me make it a little easier for you.

1) You should listen to me because I've been there, done that, and wrote a book about it. Literally.
2) You should listen to me, because no matter how easy I make these processes seem, they can be challenging and I'll

be completely transparent about the struggles I've faced on the journey as an Author.

3) You should listen to me, because I can guarantee you there is no one who is going to push you, encourage you, and hold you accountable to your goal of writing your book like I will. So, get ready.

4) You should listen to me, because if you knew the answers already then your book would be done and you wouldn't have read this far. So, don't worry. I got you. You'll be glad you picked this book up when it's all said and done.

Read This:
When You Want to Write the Book, But You Have No Clue Where to Start

It takes a lot of courage to decide that you are going to write a book. When the idea comes to you it can be both exhilarating and frightening. The urge that surfaces is one you surely do not want to surpass. Most times book ideas come to us for a reason. We may feel inspired to write about our lives, to teach something that we know, to tell a moving story, to offer advice of some sort to those we feel could benefit. We may even desire to empower people of all kinds to believe in themselves, love themselves, and never give up. These are just a few of the ideas people have come to me with when they explain that they want to write a book. As an author coach, it is my job to help these individuals figure out the message they want to share and guide them to executing it in a way that is favored by their audience.

Deciding What to Write

Sometimes when the book concept comes to you, so does the title, the theme, and the foundation of the text. Other times, when the book idea hits you, that's all it does – hit you. You find yourself stuck with the nagging revelation that you SHOULD write a book, but you're not quite sure what your book should be about, what it needs to read, or who it's even for. The first step to successfully starting your book is being clear on what you are going to write about. If the answer does not jump out at you, you may find that it will reveal itself when you go within.

Follow Your Intuition

What is your gut feeling telling you? That inner voice that told you that you need to write a book will likely be the same voice that will tell you what the book should be about. Oftentimes, we can get caught up in the overwhelming feeling of the idea of a thing that we overlook the meaning behind that thing. Think about what you have to offer. Are you a creative who has amazing stories bottled up inside your head just waiting to spill out onto pages and into the hearts of people who would appreciate your storylines? Are you the CEO of a Fortune-500 company who knows exactly how to perform your job like the professional you are, yet you do it in a sophisticated manner that is worth teaching other women how to? Maybe, you're a mother of two beautiful baby girls who struggle with the day to day acceptance of their big, naturally curly hair or their mocha chocolate skin. You want them to feel proud of who they are, where they come from, and how they look so you write a book to build their self-confidence.

Your intuition is that voice inside you that leads you to the answers of life's toughest decisions. It's the predictor of your destiny and on most occasions when you follow it, you are almost always led in the right direction.

Intuition vs. Logic

Every idea that comes to you does not have to be justified with logic. The truth is, we don't always have to make sense out of everything. Sometimes, it behooves us to just go with the flow of things. There is no difference when it comes to writing a book.

In my experience, I have found that when I neglect my intuition (what I *feel* is the right thing to write) in an effort to feed into logic (what I *think* is the right thing to write), I struggle to write at all. It feels forced if I choose the logical route and my heart is not in it. That tone that is carried through the pages of forced material does not supersede the intellect of the reader either. In other words, they peep it… and if reading forced content is hard on the writer, one can only imagine what that does for the reader herself.

Write what you feel is right. When you do this, you invite a sense of ease to your process and you will find that tackling the writing is not as difficult as it seemed when you were thinking from a logical perspective. You want to be smart when it comes to choosing the theme of your book. However, you don't want to get to the point where you are so smart that you lose all sense of creativity and passion for the project.

Research Books That Are Similar To What You Want to Write

When you identify the kind of book you want to write, it will be beneficial to do a little digging. The best writers are avid readers and this comes from the constant exposure to language and styles of writing. No one wants to read a mediocre book. Similarly, no one wants to read a book that says the same thing as the next book. The purpose of researching books that are similar to the one you want to write is to figure out what these other books failed to incorporate. You want to be able to bring a fresh perspective to your book that the next author didn't. This is what will make your book stand out from others in your genre.

Give Yourself Permission

It may sound strange - the idea of entering a bathroom and looking at the mirror on the wall to tell yourself that you give yourself permission to write this book. However, sometimes, this is the step that has to be taken to begin claiming the energy and time that will be necessary to complete the task at hand. From both a psychological and spiritual standpoint, it can be challenging to take on any new project when we haven't consulted with ourselves in a way that provides that ease and confidence needed to actually execute the assignment. Writing a book of any kind requires that the author allow a level of vulnerability to take precedence so that the best work is put forth. When we give ourselves permission to open up and be vulnerable in our writing, we create that ease we need to sustain a healthy and consistent writing routine. Giving yourself permission could simply be saying the words, *"I give myself permission to write this book,"* or *"I give myself permission to tell my story in the form of a book."* If you struggle with self-doubt or are in need of reassurance that this book is a good thing, repeat those words to yourself as often as you need to. It can and will change the scope of the journey you're about to take, before it even gets started.

Get Out of Your Head and Onto Paper

One of the initial challenges that my client's profess when they come to me is that they don't know how to get all of their thoughts out of their head. To be honest, I often laugh at that statement because the solution to that problem is as simple as 1, 2, and 3. The best way to get a hold of all the ideas going through your mind for your book is to transfer those thoughts onto paper. You literally just need to brain dump.

As you begin this journey of writing a book, you want to get a notebook or journal that will be dedicated solely to your book. You can easily grab this at your local dollar store for a dollar or less. Make this notebook sacred. Don't write anything else in it as it should serve only as your go-to for book related concepts. Once you have this notebook in place and ready to go, the first few pages should be dedicated to your thoughts. You are going to write every single thing: word, phrase, expression, memory, setting, and point that comes to your mind in these first few pages. You are going to use all of this as the foundation to drafting what will be an extensive outline that you'll follow to finish the book.

Organize Your Thoughts into an Outline

Getting your thoughts onto paper is indeed a crucial part to successfully starting your book, but the most important piece by far is organizing those thoughts and drafting an extensive outline that will guide you along the way. The worst feeling is when you're writing your book and you're excited about the newness of it all, but you haven't fully prepared for the journey. You get stuck before you even get started. More often than not, when people mention to me that they don't know where to start or they came up with a title but no content, I'm usually able to assess immediately that they have not constructed an outline. If they have created an outline, it was a very basic outline that did not quite go into deep detail about the ins and outs of each chapter or page in a way that the words would flow naturally.

What I have learned for sure is that no matter how great of a writer you think you are, no matter how many pages you were able to get through before reaching a halt, or no matter how many books you've already written – if you do not take the time to outline your book with specificity, you will find yourself spending a lot of the time you could be writing, trying to figure out what you're going to say next. Imagine the level of peace and certainty you could have if only you were fully prepared to write every inch of your manuscript without stopping. The thought alone is so enticing that it will have you wanting to get the outlining process over with as soon as possible.

Basic vs. Extensive Outline

A basic outline (where you only list the titles or themes of each chapter without going into detail) provides you with the basis for your book's flow. To jot down the main points you want to touch on eliminates the sense of feeling like you've just come up with any old thing to put in your book. It doesn't, however, keep you from pondering how much and how deep you want to write on a specific topic. It makes room for more guessing which eventually slows down the easy paced process to just writing and getting the manuscript completed. An extensive outline can be a blessing when you go so into detail, that you practically start writing complete sentences. Again, the less you have to think about while you're actually writing the book, the quicker and less strenuous the process of writing your book will be.

Decide On a Realistic Book Release Date & Create a Consistent Writing Schedule That Works for You

With every new project, you have to begin with the end in mind. Writing a book is no different. If you desire to write a book that will one day be used as the ticket for upgrading your life in any way, then you want to be very strategic from the start to the finish. Beginning your writing journey with an estimated date of completion prepares you to start operating as an author. If you've noticed, experienced writers and authors work on deadlines. When traditional publishing companies establish contracts with authors, they are given deadlines to be done with their writing. Editors are given deadlines to be done with the editing process. As well, graphic designers and illustrators are given deadlines to be done with all imaging.

In the literary industry, deadlines rule the nature of the business. Knowing that this is so, when you get clear on your book idea and once you have organized all of your thoughts into a detailed outline, you need to decide when you want your book in your hand. Whatever date you choose to have your book in your hand, your actual writing deadline should be at least a month or two prior to the actual release date. For example, this year I will be releasing my first annual birthday book. My birthday is on October

17th and I would like for my book to be in my hand on that day. In order to give my editor enough time to edit the book, and myself enough time to handle the logistics of publishing the book, I will need to be done writing the book by August 17th; and, definitely no later than September 17th.

Once you decide on a realistic deadline for you to be done writing your book, you then want to create a realistic writing schedule that will help you maintain a regular rhythm to finish by that deadline.

Example:

Zenobia decides on January 1st that she is going to write a book about dealing with mental health in the Black and Latino communities. She has already completed a brain dump, where she took one hour out of her busy schedule to write down on paper all of the thoughts traveling through her mind about her book idea. Once she jotted down all of her thoughts, she scheduled a Strategy Session with me to help her create a detailed and thorough outline for her book. After I helped her draft her outline, she proceeded to set a deadline to be finished with her book. Since, Mental Health Awareness month is in May, Zenobia figured that it would be perfect to have her book in her hand by that time to be able to promote it while the nation would be talking about Mental Health Awareness. Zenobia concluded that in order to give herself enough time to learn the publishing process and to do it right, she needed to be done with her book by March 21st.

The Breakdown:
- Zenobia starts her book on January 1st.
- She wants to be done writing by March 21st.
- January 1st to March 21st is approximately 79 days.
- Zenobia wants to reach a word count goal of 30,000 words, which is a good amount for a non-fiction book of this kind.
- She calculates that in order to reach her 30,000 word count goal by March 21st, she will need to commit to writing at least 379 words daily.

30,000 words / 79 days = 379 words per day

Identifying Your Target Audience

Your book is NOT for everybody. I repeat. Your book is NOT for everybody. Understanding this, accepting this, and being proactive in locating who your book is for will save you time, energy, money, and hurt feelings.

Figuring out who your target audience is can be quite a challenge. For me, it took almost a year of mistakes and money loss to finally figure out who my target audience was for my first book. However, once I figured it out, there was nothing stopping me from my own success. Identifying your target audience is half the battle, and the only thing to do after that is to figure out how to reach them.

If you're writing a book and you are confused about who it's for, this message is for you.

Think about the nature of your text. What kind of book are you writing? Is it fiction or non-fiction? What genre is it? If fiction, are you writing a romance novel, a drama, or a thriller? If non-fiction, are you writing your memoir, a tell-all book, a political analysis of some sort or a resource guide for your niche? In order to grasp the audience for your coming title, you have to be clear on what it is that you're writing because that is what will lead you to who. Who is it for?

Deciding what you want to write is what determines who it's for. You may be a project manager for a Nonprofit Organization and you have a wide array of knowledge and skillset that you wouldn't mind teaching other people how to obtain. You can deliver your expertise in the form of a book, including tips and strategies that have worked for you, as well as your own personal stories and experiences to help the reader relate to you. You would then package your book in such a way that it reaches the demographic of people who will most likely benefit from your book. You may market it to the audience of entry level professionals looking to do the job you do, or maybe you want to market it to other project managers who are having a difficult time balancing it all and need a little assistance with getting better organized. Again, clarity in who your book is for saves you a lot of time and money. There's nothing worse than putting your all into a book, marketing it to anybody and everybody, and never making a return on your investment. It can do something to your psyche if you allow it to, but I would rather you not even make that mistake and instead just be very clear from the start.

    You can do this by asking around. Ask your close family members and trusted friends, the people who have your best interest at heart, who won't sugar coat anything, and who will give it to you straight. Ask for assistance in identifying who your book will speak the loudest too.

Read This:
When You Have Started Writing and Stopped

I got a call not too long ago from a sister who needed me to help her get unstuck. She had started writing her book ten years ago and then, life happened. She found herself trying to pick the pen up whenever she felt led to write something, but she struggled to remain consistent in the process and it resulted in her reaching out to me nearly ten years later to pick up where she left off.

You may or may not be this woman, but if you're reading this particular section of the book I'm guessing you too have started and stopped. The question I want you to ask yourself is why? Why have you stopped writing your book? Could it be that you got so caught up in the idea of the book that you let the actual writing of the book fall to the wayside? Or, are you writing your life story and it has become too emotional to bear? Are you procrastinating and allowing this great idea of a book to just sit there and be just that… and idea? Or, are you falling victim to the myth that is "writer's block?"

Before you can move forward in writing your book, you have to understand what it is that has caused you to stop. Knowing this information will help you avoid that blockage like the plague. I want you to begin writing again because your book can and will change lives. We will never get to see what it can do though, if you don't finish it.

Push Past the Hype and Write

We live in a world where titles mean a lot to many people. For some, having a title attached to their name creates a sense of belonging and it labels them as a particular somebody. If we look at the 45th President of the United States, we can be reminded how much titles can be a dangerous thing. However, we can also take a look at Michael Jackson and what it meant to be "The King of Pop." No matter who holds the position, there is a certain level of respect that we are taught to have when individuals secure a certain title. There are those we are taught to honor, like the titles of "husband" and "wife", and then there are those that society has tricked us into believing don't really matter. Whatever the case, when it comes to the title of "Author", there can be a particular reverence that people give us because of what some may note as a tedious task to write a book.

In so many words, you have decided to write a book and you may just be feeling yourself. I can't lie. I was definitely feeling myself long before I published my first book. As a matter of fact, I was telling folks that I was the Author of a book that I hadn't even started writing yet. It's funny now looking back at how many people believed my hype before I even delivered the product. It was so easy to get acclimated to the title of Author that I almost forgot to do the work. Knowing how simple it was for me to get caught up in the hype of writing a book is all the reminder I need to know that you could potentially be doing the same thing I did.

You have to push past the hype and actually write. Sis, I only speak from experience. The book won't write itself and if you don't put the pen to paper or your fingers to the keys, your book won't get done. The most uncomfortable (and possibly embarrassing) position you can find yourself in is having someone ask you where they can get your book and you haven't even written it yet. Sure, you may be able to finagle your way around the conversation, but deep down you know you should be writing. There's not much more to it than to just do it.

The Myth of Writer's Block

It's no secret that I have stepped on a few toes on my journey in the literary industry, because I've always been very vocal about not believing in the myth that is writer's block. Personally, I believe that writer's block is simply an excuse we give when we lack the proper preparation to perform the written agenda. When you take the time to actually plan out what you will be writing about, chapter by chapter, page by page, point by point, you will find that you really have no reason to be stuck because the overall message of the book is laid out. This is why I stress drafting extensive outlines before starting books. If you desire a smooth writing experience; one where you're not wrecking your brain trying to figure out what to say next, you must get it all out of your head and organize your thoughts down to the T.

Just think about it for a second. Why do you really have writer's block? Is it that you really have no clue what to say next? Or, is it the fact that you just didn't prepare for what to say next? I'm never one to discourage anyone from writing, and especially writing a book. However, if you find that you are struggling to figure out what is next even in your outline drafting, you may need to give yourself a little bit more time before you start this book. You may need to do a little more research into what you are writing about, or you may need to simply deal with the emotions before putting the writing into motion.

Tips to Combat "Writer's Block"

As mentioned above, the real cure to the writer's block sickness is preparation, but just in case you've already outlined your book and you're still hitting a brick wall you can try these remedies.

1) Take a break. (Not a long break, but a short break from your writing to recalibrate your thoughts and center your focus back on your plan of action; the outline.)
2) Place yourself in atmospheres where you feel the energy of writing. (For example: When I am feeling uninspired, I may leave my home and go sit in Barnes & Noble, the local library, or local café to get in the zone. Being in a bookstore or library in particular have a way of building my confidence. I like to write in these spaces because as I look around and see the books, it is a reminder to me that I'll be there one day.)
3) Read other authors' books. (When all else fails and you can't find the motivation to write your own book at the

moment, take some time to read for leisure. You may find that in reading books from other authors, you will be encouraged to complete your own.)

Dealing With the Emotions

For some people, writing can be therapeutic. It can relieve us of stress, depression, and anxiety if we allow it the space to do so. This is not to say that our therapy should start and stop with writing alone. In communities of color, in particular, the idea of going to therapy to deal with our feelings, challenges, and overall mental health is something that is not looked upon as a positive or enlightening thing all the time. Granted, we are getting to a point in history where there is great pride in our culture, health and wellness. However, mental health acceptance moves at a slower pace. A lot of the times, the struggles we face that often need attention in this manner are so common that we think it's just the way of life. We as a people have been emotionally neglected, mentally, physically, and psychologically oppressed for so long that the evolution of healing seems far-fetched.

Writing texts that include memoirs, biographies, or accounts of our lives no matter how pretty or how ugly it's been can be trying and it can cause us to stop. As easy as it is for me to say, "Don't stop", it's not as simple as it seems and I understand that. Some experiences that we must mentally relive in order to tell the story can truly take a toll on us. If this is the case for you, find someone to talk to who may be skilled in assisting you with dealing with the motions that the emotions can put you through.

Stop Overthinking

One of the number one reasons why books don't get finished is because the author is overthinking. In order for you to successfully write and finish your book, you have to stop overthinking. You could be thinking about so much. Your mind could go everywhere from questioning whether you're qualified to write this book, whether or not anyone is going to read the book, or whether it's even worth the time and energy to write it. I've had clients who have literally driven themselves crazy with the thoughts of not knowing whether people would be mad at them for writing their books. I've heard so many people say they don't know their target audience, so they proceed not to write the book. Then, there are others who lack belief in their creative path. I've heard, "My imagination is a little wild. Are people going to think I'm crazy if I put this in a book?"

All of these different things that come to mind when it's time to write are simply voices in your head. What these voices in your head do is stop you from actually executing your plan to not only start, but complete the task at hand. What I've learned is that if you don't have a solid plan, you will set yourself up to overthink. That is what will happen when your thoughts are not organized.

Identify what your plan is, write out your outline, and commit to your writing schedule. At some point, you will have to get diligent and disciplined enough to just tune out the insecure voices in your head that say, I can't do this or I'm not qualified to do this or no one is going to read this. Wondering whether anyone is going to read your book is not a healthy approach to getting it done. Even if nobody reads your book but your mama or your child – still write the book, sis.

Stop Procrastinating

Procrastination is the killer of all dreams. Pertaining to writing your book, procrastination can drive its ugly head into your daily actions and literally mess up the flow of your routine. You may say, "Okay, I want to write today." Then, instead, you begin to do a plethora of other things that don't include actually writing your book. You already have a lot on your plate. You might have children to feed, a spouse or significant other you have to cater to, a full-time job you have to get up for every day, chores around the house, and all these different things that take up your time throughout the day. After having accomplished all the tasks on your to-do list, you get to the end of the day and realize you're tired – so, you make plans to "write tomorrow". Then, tomorrow comes and you do the same routine. You still don't write. Then, the next day comes and then the next day comes and then the next.

You have now succumbed to a repetitive cycle of putting off your writing. You keep saying you WANT to write or you are GOING to write, but you're not actually writing. At some point, you will have to say no more to procrastination. You have to write. You have to make the time when it doesn't feel like you have the time. You have to get stingy with your time, and let those around you know that this is important to you and you can no longer put it off for later. Life is too short to constantly put the things you desire to do off for "later". In all honesty, later may never come. You may leave this earth before your proclaimed "later date" and by then you won't have a published book to leave behind for your loved ones or the world.

Put yourself on a schedule and stick to the schedule, no matter what. Execute the plan, by any means necessary.

Stop Writing Like it is A Hobby

You are writing like it's a hobby, sis. You have to stop that. What I mean by that is, once you have decided that you're going to write a book, it is no longer a pastime. It is now a job. It is now a way that you're going to be able to finance some of your dreams. It is a way of bringing in income whether you become a full-time author or a side-hustling author. You have to stop thinking that this is something you want to do for leisure. It's leisure when you just want to write on the go or you want to write in your journal or your diary, or just write emails to people. You can do that when you're "just writing". However, when you decide that you want to become an author, or you want to write a book, you have to now put it in your mind frame that being an author is a career path. It's not writing a book just to say you wrote a book. It's adding on to your already invested career, which means you have to stop approaching it like it's a pastime and write like it's a part of the day to day.

If you get up and go to work every day at your 9-5 or in your own business, you need to allot a certain amount of time every day to writing your book. This could mean giving yourself thirty minutes to dedicate to writing on your lunch break, or even using a transcribing app on your phone and recording your words as you drive to your next location or walk on the treadmill. Start with thirty minutes a day and then challenge yourself to try and top your word count or your page count every day. When you do this, you get in the mindset and the habit that says, okay this is a major career move. This is something I'm going to do. This is someone I'm going to be. Adding "Author" to your already existing career means you have to take it just as seriously as you would any other job you do. You have to look at it like it's another way to bring money and favor into your life, for your family, for your business, and for your dreams. Stop writing like it's a hobby and you will see the growth you desire.

Stop Editing While You're Still Writing

You want to know what's funny? True story. I had to catch myself doing this very thing I'm about to speak on while writing this book. Sis, you have got to stop editing while you're still writing. (By sis, I'm speaking to myself as well.) This is probably one of the top actions that slow up the process to completion, and I'll tell you why. The urge to go back and read your work to make sure that it makes sense and things flow correctly is not at all uncommon. In fact, it is too common and it stems back to the points that were made in the section about overthinking.

As an editor, it's almost impossible for me to just write straight through my own book without going back over it to revise every opportunity I get. It has definitely been one of the hardest urges for me to conquer. I have learned though, that doing this not only slows me down but it can lead to stifling creative energy and it prolongs the process. A great writer lets go of all boundaries and just allows herself to go with the flow of her feelings and write. This experience is a beautiful thing, as it forges space to be completely artistic without restraints. This energy is suppressed when technicality comes into play and that is all that editing while writing is; a technicality.

It is okay to revise your work when you have satisfied the writing task, but it is not okay to try and go back while you're still writing and especially not when you've just begun. That's a certified recipe for stagnancy. Let your editor edit. You just need to worry about writing, or else the road to the finish line will take much longer than you projected.

Just think about it. You're writing your book. You finish a paragraph. You decide to read back over that paragraph. You're not satisfied with the paragraph you wrote, so you proceed to edit that paragraph. You make changes, add and subtract words, and then you go on to read the entire chapter. You're not satisfied with the chapter either, so now you go on to edit the entire chapter.

What is happening here? Are you writing your book, or are you butchering your manuscript? You are sabotaging your own book by disrupting the flow of the writing process with your constant editing. You want to wait to start revising once you are at least 80% done with your book.

I don't advise not editing your book. I believe every author should revise their work before sending it to me or any other editor. However, I don't believe you should be editing after every chapter, every paragraph, and every sentence. You just want to wait until you're done or very close to being done. Just write, sis. I'm an editor. This is my job. If you feel like doing my job, by all means go ahead. Just note that it may take you forever to finish your book.

Stop Doubting Yourself

If you want to make it as an author in this industry, you have to stop doubting yourself. How are you going to convince someone that your book is the shit if you don't believe it yourself? You can't expect people to believe in you if you don't even believe in you, and people can diagnose fear and insecurity easily.

The cousin to procrastination is self-doubt and just like the former, it can kill your dreams. You have to believe that what you are writing in your book is valuable and it is going to touch someone's life. If you don't believe in your book, people are not going to be convinced to buy it. They're not going to be excited to read it, and they will be hesitant in supporting your vision. In a nutshell, if you doubt yourself throughout the process, you will not succeed.

Repeat the Following Affirmations:

1) I am qualified to write this book.
2) My story is going to impact millions.
3) I have a prolific imagination that people will want to indulge in.
4) My book makes sense.
5) My book is going to change someone's life.
6) My book is worth writing.
7) My story is worth telling.
8) Writing my book will be one of the best things I ever do.

4 Ways I Remain Consistent in My Writing

1) I plan my book out from beginning to end. I leave no gaps or incomplete thoughts on the paper. A detailed outline is the major key.
2) I calendar my writing into my daily schedule. Every day I write for one hour consistently with no interruptions. To make sure I don't miss my hour a day, I put it into my schedule, set my alarm, and follow through when it's time.
3) I create my own writing haven. I have designated a room in my home for writing only. When I am ready to write for the day, I enter this room and I turn off all distracting devices (phone, tablet, television, etc.) I light my Scent Messages Candles, I burn my incense, and I may play quiet music or ocean sounds to get my mind focused on the peaceful writing session ahead.
4) I track everything! I literally track my daily, weekly, and monthly writing goals, whether I'm going on word count, page count, or just content completion. I've Tracking my goals regularly keeps me very motivated.

Read This:
When You Begin to Feel Discouraged

It happens. We get overwhelmed with the many thoughts and feelings that surface as we reflect on the journey we decided to take as authors and.... It gets discouraging. For more reasons than one, the literary exploration can be challenging when it's traveled alone. When you are surrounded by individuals who do not share the connection of being a writer, it is easy to get discouraged. Not to mention, living in a society where everything is digital (information is readily available and easily accessible via the internet) it may seem that what we have to say is not worth putting in a book. Don't be fooled. There is definitely always room for another author and another book in this lifetime.

Reflect on How Far You've Come

Whether you're in the beginning stages of your book, you're halfway through, or you're almost done, I want you to take a moment to just cerebrate on your course thus far. It doubtlessly takes a tremendous amount of courage to not only make the determination to write a book, but to actively take steps to enact the plan of action. You should be proud of your audacity to strive for more than just the intention of writing a book.

Remember Your Why

When you find yourself feeling the daunting apprehension of writing and releasing your book to the masses, take a moment to reflect on your why. Why are you writing this book? What led you to the realization that you needed to write a book? Who are you doing this for? Is this book going to mean something in the long run or is this not for you? What is your why?

When I wrote *Young Black Fearless*, my "why" is what drove me to becoming a grassroots bestseller, an award winner, and a keynote speaker. I wanted that book to do many things, but more than anything, I wanted to provide young people of color a solution based book to activism. During the time of its release, the officer that had shot and killed Mike Brown was just exonerated, a year prior George Zimmerman had gotten off for murdering Trayvon Martin, and we were still trying to figure out who killed Kendrick Johnson. I was angry, like many of my peers in the activist scene. We were sick and tired, heartbroken, and mad as hell. I clearly saw where our rage was keeping us up at night in the name of justice, but I also saw that our diligence and relentless resistance was finally starting to pay off, particularly in cases in the Atlanta area. I wrote *Young Black Fearless* with the intentions of teaching other young activists across the country how to strategically organize in a way that merited results.

The second part to my "why" for that book was so that I could dispel the myth that Black Lives Matter activists and organizers didn't "know what they wanted" or "were only good for causing chaos without any clear demands". Now, I have never been a part of the Black Lives Matter organization, but I've been a leader in the movement itself since the death of Mike Brown. People often could not differentiate who was in the organization as opposed to who was simply a participant in the movement for black lives. Due to this misunderstanding, I spent a great deal of energy during that time debating on radio stations, public forums, and even in my college classrooms. I was to the point where I was tired of always having to defend the movement and the work of organizers like myself, that I wrote a book. That book made a statement that not many could argue with because I was able to really break it down for folks to understand that what they chose to believe (because they weren't on the front lines with us) was merely an ignorant assumption. It was my "why" in this book that pushed me to completion. It will be your "why" that will push you to do the same for your book.

Think About Who It Will Benefit

I'm going to be honest here and say that this book, *Write the Book, Sis!* was totally not planned. Sure, I knew that eventually I wanted to elaborate on the eBook I published early in 2017 that talked about writing books, but I didn't think I'd be writing a book about writing books specifically for women.

The crazy thing was, I had made the decision around my birthday that I was going to change the scope of my audience in my business. For years I had been offering my services as an author coach, editor, and publisher to all people; man, woman, and teens. However, after I did my end of the year birthday business audit, I quickly realized that I had allowed several men to waste my time and energy without paying for the work I had done. Of course I was hot when I noticed all the unpaid balances and lack of responses via email and phone from the brothers I had done work for on their books. I decided in that moment that I would not market to men anymore, because I just didn't have the time or energy to fight to get paid anymore. My most loyal client base had proven to be women of color, and has recently expanded to women from all walks of life, so in turn I've chosen to go hard for women.

It wasn't until I got back on Twitter and started my LIVE Series on Instagram that I noticed how well women were taking to the hashtag #WriteTheBookSis. It seemed that out of nowhere, the support came in boatloads. I was getting emails, text messages, DMs, PMs, and comments filled with messages of support, gratitude, and declarations to write books. I knew immediately that the book about writing books needed to come sooner than later. All of the private messages that I was responding to, answering excess questions, were the foundation to these chapters you're now reading.

I figured that if woman could benefit from this information, then I could kill several birds with one stone and make the information available to more sisters than I could count. I thought about who would benefit from this book, and here we are. Thinking of the sisters who need this book is the fuel that has kept me writing in the moments when I just didn't feel like it, or I felt like there were other things I could be working on instead. Sometimes, that tribe that's waiting for you to deliver will be the very people who will sustain you on the journey.

It's easier than it seems.

Writing is the easy part. The tough part comes when it's time to publish and market your book to make the money back that you invested. You can really do this, sis. I'm not just saying it to sound cliché either. Just focus on the great things that can and will come out of this book when you change your mindset. Taking the writing process one day at a time, one page at a time, and one word at a time eliminates the anxiety that can surface when we overthink.

Consider Your Legacy

I've said this before, and I'll say it again. Leaving behind a book is leaving behind your legacy. A book can be left for your family and for the generations to come so that no one is confused about who you were, what role you played in society, and what contributions you left to the world. It's imperative that we write and publish books, to document history, and to provide the needed insight for those whom our books are written for. If nothing else helps you to remain encouraged throughout the development of your text, appreciate the end result; that which will be the legacy you leave behind when you transition into the next life.

Read This:
When Your Book is Almost Complete

The feeling of being close to the finish line can be a mix of joy, pleasure, anxiety, and fear. All the emotions you encompass as you type the final pages to your book are all natural. It's completely okay to feel nervous and excited all at the same time. This is a great thing, sis! You are literally one step closer to having a published title to your name! Of all the many things I have achieved in this lifetime and the accomplished feelings that they bring, I can honestly say that there are not too many things that top the feeling of relief when I type "THE END" at the end of a manuscript.

Now that you're reaching that threshold of achievement, it is time to begin marketing yourself as an author. It's time for you (if you haven't already) to start letting it be known that you have a book on the way so your family, friends, followers, and fans will begin to prepare to spend money on that book when it releases. The goal is to market hard before the book is released so that when it comes out, you don't have to work as hard. As mentioned before,

I'm the Queen of working smarter and not harder. I've tested out this strategy of marketing at least two months (one month at the latest) before release day, so that on the day the book becomes available, sales come in easily. Trust me when I say it has definitely worked well for me!

One of the things that I hear often from people who are fearful of beginning the marketing process is that "no one knows who I am". Though that might be the case, it won't be the case for long if you change your mindset and follow the instructions I am about to give.

You Have to Pay to Play

Like any business, campaign, or product, it costs money to make money. Just as it takes money to front for the self-publishing process, it will also cost money (oftentimes more in the long run) to market your book and yourself as an author. But, before we get into all the costs and expenses that will arise in the marketing arena, I want to break down some of the simple and inexpensive ways to begin marketing yourself and your book before it releases.

Free Social Media Marketing

In the age of social media you should know by now that there is almost nothing you can't do. This includes preparing a platform for people to follow your journey as an author and to get information on your book(s). You may already have a page on all social media platforms, but as you prepare for your book to come, you want to either (1) create a professional author page or book page, or (2) customize your existing pages to display your author/book information. Here are the necessary components to setting your social media up:

Create a Free Facebook Business Page

Facebook allows its users to create both a personal page and a business page. When you are establishing yourself as an author, you want to be able to send your readers and supporters to your business page rather than accepting friend requests from people you may not know, or may not want to invite into your personal space. Your business page will be a page that supporters and readers can "like" to stay connected to your author brand. This page will serve as a spring board for all things related to your upcoming book.

Create a Free Instagram Page

Instagram is an excellent platform to promote your book and to establish yourself as an authority in your arena if you use it properly. It is a photo driven platform so you could use it to post pictures of your book, quotes related to your book (you can use www.canva.com to create images for your brand), and even professional pictures of you to market your book. Keep in mind, beauty sells! It's always a good look to put on some makeup and have someone take some nice photos of you to promote.

Create a Free Twitter Page

Twitter is the platform where you get things off of your chest. It is one of the first social media platforms that only allowed you to "tweet" i.e. post words, messages, and quotes as a means of connecting. You can use this platform to share quotes and small excerpts from your book. You can also talk directly to your readers and it'll post to your page to show you are engaging. This platform is also good to tweet or retweet media coverage that relates to the theme of your book, or provides talking points to encourage conversation that is book related.

Create a Free YouTube Page

As all of these platforms are optional to use, you still want to setup accounts for all. YouTube is by far the number one social media platform and it is video driven. This program allows you to have your own channel where you can record videos that are related to your book and author brand. You could do Q&A's for your readers, offer book club discussion questions, offer a behind the scenes exclusive of what it took to create the book, and simply introduce yourself to people who may not know who you are.

Create a posting schedule to post different things about your book.

Once you have identified the free social media sites you want to take advantage of, you want to focus on branding those sites in a way that lets people know it's you. I have seen often that authors will have many different looks across all of their social media platforms and it can be confusing for people. You want to make sure that the brand colors you use, the information you share, and the links and directions to purchasing or preordering your book remain consistent across all boards. You want to make it easy for people to find you and follow you across the spectrum and not make it difficult to figure out what it is you're doing. I learned this the hard way, so I understand how important this is.

Next, you want to work on building a following. This can be done by following other people whose pages spark intrigue for you, reposting and retweeting folks who have shared some good information, something funny, or cute. You can use hashtags to find people to follow on Instagram and also help them to find you. Research hashtags that are related to your book's topic or even use hashtags related to being an author. The more you use hashtags, the better chances you have of being discovered on any of the social media search engines. I've been able to really build my following from strategic usage of hashtags.

Lastly, you want your posts to be engaging. Posts can be: quotes from the book, small passages, and pictures related to your book, book giveaways, quick videos about why people should purchase your book, etc. BE CREATIVE!

Final Month Countdown

The last month BEFORE your book release, you should post something EVERY DAY! One of the things you definitely want to do is change your profile pictures (on all platforms) to your book cover. This way, people will know for a fact that the reason you're posting so frequently is because you have a book coming out.

Email Marketing

If someone were to ask me what has been the greatest form of marketing for me, it would most definitely be email marketing. Collecting emails and creating more intimate relationships with (tribe) is how I've been able to sell out my books from the online perspective. Every author should have an email list. As well, every author should be working toward building that email list on a daily basis.

When you decide to create your mailing list to begin marketing via email, you want to do it as close to right as possible to save yourself the headache of manual labor. The number one FREE email marketing program is Mail Chimp and it is what I used for the first two years of my journey as an author. Mail Chimp easily integrates with almost every website hosting program and it makes it super accessible for potential subscribers to simply leave their emails and it convert directly to your list with ease. Mail Chimp is free for the first 1,000 subscribers and is a great option for first time authors. Visit www.mailchimp.com to configure your lists and set yourself up right.

Quick Tip: Remember that every event you go to where you're either selling your book or promoting your book, it's always a good idea to keep a sheet of paper or an open note tab on your phone available so that you can take emails on the go and manually add folks you meet into your email list.

Create an opt-in email list and set-up automated emails to get comfortable with new subscribers before selling book.

An opt-in is a fancy term used to describe the attention grabber that you will present to people in exchange for their email. You want to build your email list and a surefire way to do this is by offering something potential readers may be interested in, to in turn get their email added to your email list. That email list is going to be your best friend, as it will serve as the most direct form of communication to readers and supporters. One of the things you can offer your growing email subscribers is a free chapter or a teaser of your book. That's what I did with this book, and it built my email list beyond what I could have imagined. When you designate a specific chapter to your book for the opt-in freebie, you will not only gain new fans of your writing, but you will also build a level of trust because many people will feel like this person must be on it if they are giving away a whole free chapter. You also want to make sure that the chapter or teaser section that you offer your potential subscribers is the best of the entire book. You want to win them over, and you will have a hard time doing so if you choose to be stingy and give away the least interesting aspect of your book for free. Be smart. Give up the best of the goods and it will have people not only rushing to join the email list, but also ready to preorder and secure their copy!

Once you've set up your opt-in offer, you will see on your email hosting service that there is an option to automate emails. This means that you can pre-write emails to be sent to your audience as soon as they join your email list. It will seem like you are so on top of your game that you responded to someone joining your email list, right away and directly. However, in most cases, those immediate email replies are simply automated messages that have been created to keep you on your toes. Some email hosting platforms allow you to create automations for free, while others may request that you upgrade from your free account to a monthly paid account. You don't HAVE to start automating right away. In fact, I would recommend holding off on automation until you begin to get so many subscribers that you can't keep up.

I must say though, automation comes in handy because it truly sets you up in a way that allows you to focus on other things. Email marketing can get to be overwhelming, simply because for most people that is where the sales are made. You have to consistently touch your subscribers if you want them to buy with you and that takes more than one email, which is why email automations are exactly what you need in those instances. You can create an automated email that welcomes your new subscriber and makes her feel at home. You can send another automated email a day or two later introducing who you are and maybe sharing something special or important about you so the subscriber now feels like they know you a little better. You can literally create a series of automated emails to deliver to the inbox of your new subscriber every other day leading up to your book launch date. You want to be on their minds, not out of sight and out of mind. One of the best ways to do this (aside from your social media presence) is by sending these emails.

Choose a day or two out of EACH week to send an email to your subscribers. Your emails can fall in line with your social media posts.

Should you choose not to automate your emails or if you would like to keep your subscribers abreast on a weekly basis, you definitely want to send out an email campaign or broadcast at least one or two times out of each week leading up to your book release date. Your emails can fall in line with your social media posts, or it could be conversational based where you're just writing to "check-in" and maybe you can ask that your subscribers reply back to your email to let you know that they are actively reading your emails. Doing so will hopefully serve an encouraging factor where you will be reminded that your efforts to reach your audience and stay connected are not in vain.

Website Marketing

Make sure you have a website as a home base for visitors to join your mailing list. In order for your tribe to subscribe to your email list online, you need to have a website setup or some sort of online web hosting service that will allow you to collect emails. My personal favorite website hosting service is Squarespace because it is setup to make the website building technique extremely straightforward and painless for folks who are not tech savvy, like me. Using this particular platform, you can simply drag and drop what you need on your page to begin collecting emails, taking preorders, and keeping your readers and supporters abreast of everything related to your book's release.

Securing a Domain

Before or during the process of creating a website using Squarespace or any other platform, you want to make sure that you secure the domain for your site. The web address that you'll be sending people to is just as important as the site in itself. Though I mentioned before that each social media platform allows you to have your own page or space, you still want to establish yourself as close to professional as possible. This way, people will take you and your work very seriously. I've seen many authors not reach the levels of success that they could because they solely depend on their Facebook Page to send potential readers and buyers to without investing in a real website and domain name.

When deciding on a domain name, you should consider two things. Most authors create domains for themselves as an author, or for their book directly. Personally, depending on what your book is about, you may want to consider doing both.

If you are an author who aspires to write several titles, you may want to consider creating a domain name for yourself as an author. Example: www.yourname.com or www.authoryourname.com Depending on what your titles are about (if you plan to use your books as a springboard to sell other products or services) you may want to secure the book's domain name in addition to your own author domain. Example: www.yourbooktitle.com

Setting your domains up to have a home for not only yourself as an author and your book title is a great thing, as it shows the seriousness of protecting what is yours. Even if you don't necessarily want to have an active hosting site for both domains, you could always create one website and link both of your domains to that website. For example, if I want to create my website for www.authormyname.com and I wanted this website to be my go-to, I could still purchase the domain www.mybooktitle.com and link it to www.authormyname.com. This way, when people are looking up my book and they type into the search bar, www.mybooktitle.com it will send them to www.authormyname.com, which is essentially where I want my readers and supporters to show up.

Create a promotional pop-up on website to invite visitors to join your mailing list. (See Email Marketing)

As mentioned in the email marketing section above, you want to have a place on your website to collect emails for your email list. My personal favorite option is setting up a promotional pop-up so when visitors come to my website, they can scroll down a few seconds and a pop-up will automatically show up on their screen asking if they want to join my mailing list. The promotional pop-up option on Squarespace is already available to you if you visit the settings tab and then go to the marketing tab from there. It is my understanding that the Squarespace email collections are directly in sync with Mail Chimp, you just have to sign in with your credentials and choose which list you would like for added names and emails to go into. It's super simple.

Create a blog in alignment with your book and write blog posts to attract visitors to your website, to join your mailing list, and eventually purchase book.

One of the ways you can begin building traction and excitement around your book AND mailing list, is by using your website as an opportunity for you to blog. Whether you take bite sized pieces of your book's themes and write up a simple 300-500 word blog post about it to peak potential readers' interest, or you offer a free chapter of your book by way of your blog OR mailing list freebie, this is another way you can both build your email list and grow your overall audience. The name of the game is to get emails, as emails serve as a more personal and direct form of communication with potential readers and customers. Your blog can serve the purpose of gathering more like minded individuals your way.

You don't want to dilute the purpose of your blog to just a way to secure emails, either. Although it is a sure way of doing so, you want to also create an accessible online space for folks who may not know of or aren't able to purchase your book right away to still stay up on and be influenced by your writing. It would behoove every author to show their writing material outside of just books, to turn non-believers into believers. Having a solid blog that shows off your skilled and phenomenal writing ability will make it that much easier for people to spend money on your writing. Believe it or not, many people (who don't know you) may be skeptical of spending money with you if you haven't proven to a) know what you're talking about (non-fiction authors), or b) show your creative writing talents elsewhere first (fiction authors).

<u>Set up your 3D book cover as a product on your website and begin taking pre-orders. (This could also offset printer costs.)</u>

One of the key things to do while establishing the website, domains, mailing lists and such is to have your graphic designer (or yourself if you are savvy) to create your book cover and 3D mock-up. As a matter of fact, I may need to rewind and be clear that your book cover's completion is really one of the FIRST things you want to have done when it comes to starting the marketing journey for your book. You can't really convince people that you're an author of a book if they haven't or cannot see a visual of the book cover. That is why it is literally imperative to start with your book cover and use that cover as a promotional device across all platforms.

The real reason you want to get that book cover solid before anything else, is because once you do make the announcement to your people that you have written (or are writing) a book of any kind, you want to be able to send them somewhere. This of course is where your website comes in. You want to be able to direct your supportive traffic to your website which will have the photo mock-up of your book cover and you might want to begin taking preorders ahead of time.

Preorders or Not?

In my personal opinion founded off of my own experience, preorders are life savers. Okay, maybe that's a bit dramatic – but it's true ESPECIALLY if you are self-publishing. The process to self-publish your book can be quite a task and it can even be frustrating in the event that you don't have a lot of money to front the costs and expenses it takes to get the book done. Preorders can alleviate a lot of that financial stress because the coins that are collected from the preorders can actually be used toward printing costs. With my first book, I did not take preorders because I didn't quite have the time. Though as an experienced author now, writing and publishing a book in 10 days isn't much of a big deal anymore because I've learned how the process works and can do it in my sleep at this point. However, at that time there were so many things I had to learn in those 10 days that I didn't even have time to learn how to or what could preorders do for my book. Needless to say, if I could go back and try the pre-order thing, I most definitely would! In my latter books, it has literally been preorder funds added onto my own investment to get me started off in the right direction.

 The most important thing you want to keep it mind once your website has been established is updating it regularly. You want to create some sort of posting schedule, just as you would for your social media platforms. These updates on your websites should include your book launch day, your book signing events, speaking engagements (if you're going that route), your sales page, blog, photos of events, and even screenshots of book reviews and testimonials should go on your site. The goal is to flex for folks who don't know who you are yet. It takes a lot to convince people in this day and age that what you have written and what you have to say is worth reading. Knowing this, you want to be extremely strategic about how you market and promote your book, as oftentimes your marketing and promotion (if done right) will sell your books to people who will buy them by the boatload, and distribute them to their various organizations and communities.

Paid Promotions

Quite a few authors I've spoken to in the past have confessed shying away from paid promotions. I always wonder why when I've seen what paid promotions have done for me, but I understand also that some just don't have the funds to invest in paid promotions. My tip for you is to find the money, sis. You will need a marketing and promotions budget anyway, so make sure there is enough to not only establish your website, domains, and all of that, but to also run ads on a platform or several.

Interesting thing, I have run ads on mostly all social media sites just to see which one works best for me or offers the best results, yet none of the sites we've grown accustomed to seeing ads on have worked for me. Personally, I've tried a Facebook Ad and have actually designed an entire book launch funnel for this platform, yet all it brought me were new people to like my page but nothing further. I haven't given up on Facebook yet though, I'm actually determined to try and figure out their setup because I've heard of way too many success stories to not be included in any of them.

I've also tried running ads through Instagram's ad promotions (which are now in sync with Facebook). I just knew I would have a winner here as Instagram is easily my favorite and most frequented social media page. However, I was highly disappointed in the results of the IG ads I'd placed. I found myself spending more money for less time, and still getting nothing more than a measly like on my page. Now, don't get me wrong – some people live for "likes". For me though, if these likes are not converting into email subscribers to lead to potential sales, I can do without them.

What I have found to work for me though, is actually researching direct Instagram pages that share the audience I am seeking to reach. For example, after doing my research to find an audience that targeted women of color ages 26-48, I paid the owner of a well-known page that had over 260K followers to post my ad so that I could attract some of their followers my way. IT WORKED! The very first time I tried this method, I received not only 500 new followers, but I also gained about 72 new email subscribers from that 500. To me, that was a WIN! It had done much more than all the money I spent and lost with Facebook and

Instagram, even with the targeting. I was able to reach the exact audience I was looking to pour into, and I'm still gaining subscribers from the initial post.

There is really no right or wrong answer for paid promotions. It's more like a trial and error process. What works for one author, may not work for the next and I learned this by trying them all out and closely calculating and comparing the results. Listed below are several paid promotions that you may want to try to see if they work for you.

- Create a Facebook Ad via Facebook Business Page
- Create an Instagram Ad via Facebook Business Page of Instagram Business Page
- Create a Twitter Ad
- Create a Radio or Television Commerical/Ad (This may be more expensive and more difficult to pitch, but it could be worth it depending on your area.)
- Create an ad for a podcast show or ask to sponsor a show for a popular blogger or YouTube vlogger to have your book highlighted on their channel.
- Seek out social media pages/brands catering to your target audience who offer advertising for small fees. Create a quick ad (photo or video) to send, along with a caption that presents a call to action, for them to share on their page.

- Keep in mind that all of your ads should either invite people to preorder, purchase, or share the news about your new book.

Read This:
When You Are Ready to Publish Your Book

Welcome to the big league! Once you have finished writing your book, naturally the next step is to prepare for publishing. Before you move into the publishing phase though, you need to be aware of the different types of publishing options that are available to you as you want to weigh all your options before proceeding. The publishing aspect of the journey may or may not cost you money, but it all depends on the approach you take. In a nutshell, you have the option to either 1) Sign with a traditional publishing company, 2) Self-Publish your book on your own, or 3) Partner Publish with someone like me.

Traditional Publishing

This here is no secret. Traditional publishing has been around since the beginning of time. Traditional publishing companies have a history of vetting out writers as potential authors, signing them to contracts that state they are committed to authoring a set number of books in a set number of years. Oftentimes, these traditional publishing companies offer authors an advance (compensation) once they have written the book, then they (most times) take full ownership of the author's written material, they copyright it in the company's name and for the most part, they decide on the outcome of that author's book.

Some traditional publishing companies may have in the contracts you sign that they will set you up on a book tour, take care of all means of production for the book, they will help you get on platforms to speak and share your book with the world, and so on and so on. There are other traditional publishing companies that will do nothing more than post about your book the week of its release. Considering the times we're in where social media presences are what drive the nation, traditional publishing companies have definitely gotten lazy when it comes to putting in the leg work of helping their authors gain the visibility they often deserve.

The Process of Getting Signed

Much like the music industry, there is a process to getting signed by a major publication. Most traditional companies will let potential authors know when they are accepting submissions to be published, and then there are others that accept manuscripts year-round. Typically, the process entails you submitting your manuscript (it could be a few chapters or in its entirety) and waiting for an approval or denial phone call or letter. Some companies make it clear what type of manuscripts they are looking forward to receiving and others will accept anything. It is imperative that if you choose to seek out a traditional publishing company to do your research on the type of books they typically release. What kind of authors are they used to publishing? By conducting this investigation before submitting your work, you will save yourself some time, energy, and hurt feelings if they choose not to grant you a publishing contract.

 Oftentimes when individuals decide they want to write and publish a book, they have dreams of getting signed to a major traditional publishing company that will advance them a $15-$20,000 check upfront, cover all the necessary costs to get it in print, set them up on a national book signing tour, and then automatically become a New York Times Bestselling Author. Nine times out of ten, this is not the reality of many authors who submit their manuscripts to big time publishers. In fact, the process is much more challenging than it seems. Now days with social media making it extremely easy for writers to gain a following and accessibility to their fans, publishing companies take that into consideration when choosing to sign you. In other words, if you don't already have a large following on social media or a strong presence in the industry already, they will likely not want to bring you on if they think your work is average on top of all of that. They will invest in someone who has already established a fan base because that saves them some coins. If they don't think they will have to work as hard to sell your book, you are more likely to be invested in.

Royalties

One of the downfalls of traditional publishing is the distribution of royalties. These publishing companies don't give you large advances for nothing. They offer these coins to literally take ownership of your project. They may pay for your editor, graphic designer, agent, publicist, etc. but you will have to pay them back for all of those costs. These expenses are paid for from the book sales. By the time the price of a book pays its fair share to all the necessary parties involved (the publisher, the distributor, the editor, the designer, the printer, the publicist, and so on), you as the author may not receive anything. If you do receive something, it may be very little money per book.

For Example: Carina published a book with a major publishing house. Her book is being sold in stores for $16.99. Her takeaway from each book sold is only $.99. Why?
The publisher is taking 40%, which is $6.79.
The distributor is taking 35%, which is another $5.94
The expenses it cost to edit, design, and print each book equals $3.27 (really more, but they may or may not let it slide.)
Carina only walks away with $.99 per book sold.

She sales 2,500 books in one month and receives $2,475.00 in addition to her $5,000 advancement check. Altogether, she has acquired roughly $7,475.00 within her first month with this publishing company. But, before you begin to think that's a lot of money in a month let's take a look at self-publishing.

Self-Publishing

Let me start this section by stating, I am a proponent of self-publishing. The book industry has changed in that Self-Publishing has become the new wave that many authors are now riding. This form of publishing is rather self-explanatory, as it simply is the act of you investing your time, energy, money, and resources to bring your book project to fruition. Many authors have chosen to go the independent route to publishing their books for the sake of ownership of their work and the rights to use their work however they choose. Much like the music industry and politics in general, it's not uncommon to have to alter your image in a way that is deemed as appropriate or saleable to the audience in which you're trying to reach. Independent self-published authors get to be fully in control of their image, the way their work is displayed and distributed, and ultimately they get to call the shots.

    Before I became an author myself, I served as the editor for quite a few independent authors who wanted to do things their own way. I was one of those people who had dreams of being signed to a major traditional publisher with hopes of making it "big" and having my books everywhere, until I saw what self-publishing was able to do for my clients. To say the least, I was inspired immensely. To see my clients make executive decisions on how they would write, publish, market and promote their books, all while being themselves completely from beginning to end and not switching up to be someone they weren't for the sake of "making it" was exactly what I desired. I've always known deep down that I needed to own whatever my name was attached to because my name is important, as all of ours are. Some people are okay with doing things under anyone's leadership and that's okay because not everyone has the confidence, time, energy, resources, or finances that it takes to make self-publishing work for them and that is okay. It really is.

There is no right or wrong answer with how you publish, it's just a matter of what you are willing to deal with. If you are merely flirting with the idea of self-publishing, you must know that it is going to cost you money upfront to make your book happen. There are no advances when you're self-publishing. You have to put in the work and front the money to make it happen, and that is something that turns authors off at times – but like anything worth having, you've got to pay to play. It takes money to make money, especially independent money that you don't have to share with an entire company.

Example:

Bianca decided to self-publish her book rather than sign on with a major publication company that vetted her work. She invested roughly $2,000.00 in getting her book published, which included her editor, graphics, beginning marketing and promotions costs, and her first print run of books. After releasing her book for $16.99, she was able to sell the same 2,500 books as Carina, yet she was able to pocket $40,475.00 after paying herself back from the $2,000 she invested in the project to begin with.

Partner Publishing

As mentioned, there is traditional publishing (where a writer signs a contract with an established publishing company), self-publishing (where a writer takes sole responsibility in producing their own book), and recently partner publishing (where the writer and publishing company work together to bring a manuscript to life creating a memorable book and brand).

Partner publishing is not as new as people may believe that it is. In fact, quite a few printing companies have offered partner publishing as a service, although it hasn't quite been labeled as such. Essentially, when you decide you want to partner with a publishing company to publish your book, you are looking to gain the resources and expertise from said publisher to execute the job, however the book will be published in your own name. Publishers who offer this service most times offer the same variables included, however some can offer what others can't.

Partner Publishing with my company, YBF Publishing, LLC.

Choosing to partner with YBF Publishing to birth your book baby is one of the best decisions you'll make on your road to becoming an author. Not only do I offer every necessary requirement to fully publishing a book, but I teach you the process of publishing on your own if you plan to publish more books or are interested in starting your own publishing company in the future. I'll hold your hand throughout the entire process of becoming a published author and unlike traditional publishers, your book will be published in YOUR NAME/COMPANY NAME in partnership with YBF Publishing, LLC. You own ALL rights and I take NO money from your book sales.

What's Included

- Book Editing
- Book Cover Design
- Print Formatting
- An Illustrator (You Select Your Illustrator, I Connect You)
- Book Copyright Registration
- ISBN #, Barcode, Library of Congress #
- EBook Formatting (Kindle, Nook, PDF)
- Basic Author/Book Website
- Initial Book Print Run
- Initial Local Bookstore Signing Setup (Book Launch Party Planning is Not Included)
- Pre-Marketing & Initial Distribution For Your Book

The Partner Publishing Standard Package includes all of the above services listed, including your first print run. However, each author's needs are different. For instance, some authors come to me with book covers already designed or editing already completed. In this case, the price will be tailored to your specific needs. If Partner Publishing is something you are interested in doing with me or wanting to learn more about, please feel free to email me directly: editor@theliteraryrevolutionary.com and I will be glad to assist you.

Read This:
If You Decide to Self-Publish Your Book

There are several steps you need to take in order to successfully self-publish your book. I would tell you that before you get started, you need to research everything there is to know about the self-publishing business. Lucky for you, I am going to take this chapter to break down everything you need to know so that (hopefully) you won't have to search around for the answers. I am going to chop everything I have learned about publishing books into bite sized pieces so you can tackle them one by one.

Before we get into it, I want to make note that some of these steps can be done simultaneously as you're still writing your book. As a matter of fact, I encourage some of these steps be done early on in your writing journey as it will make this thing even more real than it feels. You are going to be an amazing and powerful self-published author. Your book is going to get into the hands of many people who are going to praise God and thank you for sharing your material. Get ready, this is only the beginning.

Described below are the many things you will need to check off the list to make sure you have completed all the steps to profitably publishing your book. Follow these steps and see the results of your hard work. I can promise you that even if it feels challenging, it is worth it.

<u>Step One: Identify Your Book Release Date</u>

This step is actually something you would want to accomplish long before you get to the publishing phase of things. I briefly touched on this in the starting chapter, because it's so important to begin with the end in mind. If you are writing and don't know when you want to be done, you will be writing forever. I do understand though, that some people were not taught that beforehand so if this is you, here is the opportunity to set your date. You're done with your book and at this point it's time to publish. It's also during this time of getting your book ready for print or electronic publishing that you should be marketing your book as well.

In order to market your book, you need to know when your book will be available to the public. Knowing this information will keep you committed to a deadline so that you take this self-publishing process as seriously as you would any other project you've ever been assigned. Keep in mind that self-publishing your book is almost like starting a new business. You are your boss. You set your deadlines, and you will be fronting the costs to fulfill your dreams.

Step Two: Establish the Publishing Company Name

Speaking of operating as a business... If you do not already have an established business of your own, you may want to consider securing an official name for your publishing company. If you are someone who sees themselves writing more than one book in the future, it would be a smart move to go ahead and establish a name to start using as it relates to the books you will publish. If you are someone who has no plans to write more than one book (although you never really know until you publish the first one) then you might want to focus on just using your name. You CAN do this. Independent Authors who don't desire to establish a full blown publishing house or don't want to mix their established business with the book business often times just publish their books in their name.

Examples:

Two of my Partner Publishing clients took two different routes with their publishing names. Both clients owned their own businesses and both businesses were somewhat correlated to the topics of their books. However, one of my clients decided to publish the book as an imprint under her company, and the other decided to just publish her book under her name. Either option is absolutely fine. You don't HAVE to formulate a business name with the Secretary of State's office right away either. Depending on your state's regulations, you may be able to wait until you reach a number of years in business or make a certain amount of money before registering

Step Three: Purchase an ISBN# (or Several)

This step here is critical. Your ISBN # or the "International Standard Book Number" is your book's Social Security Number. It Is the number that people can look up to distinguish your book from another. When bookstores or libraries want to look for your book to potentially place it in their facilities, they will need you to have an ISBN number readily available, or else, your book will not be considered "official".

You can acquire an ISBN number from a few different places. There are printing companies that sell ISBN numbers and you can also retrieve a free ISBN from Amazon's Createspace if you choose to sell your book on Amazon. With all the options out there for securing an ISBN, you still should only go to one source and that is the ISBN agency or (www.isbn.org). The reason you should go straight through the agency is because there are companies that literally bootleg ISBN numbers.

I'm so serious. You know when you go to a big game or a concert and there are people near the facility or on the street trying to sell you some tickets before you get to the box office? There is a chance that those tickets might be invalid, may have the wrong date or time on them, or it's been scanned already and can't be reused. The ISBN # hustle happens the same way and there are individuals and businesses out there that will try and sell you a used or invalid ISBN number. You don't want to put yourself in position to lose any money when you're self-publishing. The less money lost on this journey, the better.

There are also companies that offer real ISBN numbers that come with stipulations. Amazon's Createspace is one of those companies that get people every time. Createspace will offer you an irresistibly free ISBN number, but they put in the fine print that once you accept this ISBN number, it can only be used on their platform. This means if you choose to host your book on any other online platform, be it Barnes & Noble, Ingram Spark, or any other print on demand platform, you will run the risk of your book being snatched from Amazon. They have a strict policy that if your book is found on any other online platform using their assigned ISBN number, your book will be removed from their platform, your ISBN number will be confiscated, and you will not be able to use Createspace again. I can tell you right now that with Amazon being the wealthiest and most frequented business in the U.S. right now, the one thing you don't want to do is NOT be able to use their platform. My suggestion is that you purchase your ISBN number from (www.isbn.org) for only $135 and apply it to all platforms that will host your book.

 Another thing you want to keep in mind is that if you have plans to publish more than one book, it would be smarter (and cheaper) to purchase an ISBN number package from the agency. They offer independent authors and publishers the opportunity to purchase one number, ten numbers, or one hundred numbers at a time. These packages definitely save you money in the long run especially if you know for a fact that you will be publishing more.

Step Four: Have Book Edited By a Professional

When you are done with your book, get ready to reach out to myself or other editors in the industry to work magic on your manuscript. The job of the editor is to make sure your book is solid and ready for print. This includes proofreading your work, adding a little copy here and there, and even ghostwriting if necessary. We refine all of your grammar, punctuation, sentence structure and surface level issues, and fine-tune the content of your message so that it all makes sense and can be easily read without obstruction.

In most cases, an editor is necessary and it is an investment that could make all the difference from being a non-selling author to becoming a bestselling author. This is not necessarily the time to have your cousin's step-sister's boyfriend's mama's cousin's great-grandson's baby mama looking over your book. There are editors that offer different ways of measuring their work and retrieving payment. Some will charge by the word count, page count, or a flat rate. This area of publishing is not one that you want to be cheap about because mediocre or confusing writing could cost you your reputation before you even really get started. If you are interested in having me edit your manuscript, feel free to email me directly: editor@theliteraryrevolutionary.com

Step Five: Design Your Book Cover

Your book cover should be designed sooner than later. To be honest, it's something you want to get done almost as soon as you've decided on a book title. You can hire a graphic designer by searching for them on google, looking for someone on www.fivr.com, asking your Facebook friends, or seeking a referral. If push comes to shove and you are unable to find someone to do it within your budget, go to www.canva.com which is a website which will assist you in making an easy and free book cover.

Step Six: Have your book formatted for print and eBook

In some cases, you will not have to go any further to have your book formatted for print or eBook when you're working with a skilled editor. If they are anything like me, they will include formatting in their editing rates, or will offer the service separately. If you do not have an editor who can also format the book, you will want to hire a typesetter or watch a few YouTube videos that will teach you how to get your book print ready. A regular Microsoft Word document with no alterations specific to your uploading needs will not suffice.

Step Seven: Decide on a price point and generate a barcode

Once your book has been edited by a professional, you will need to secure a barcode to go with your ISBN number. The reason you want to wait until your book has been edited is because during this stage you are going to price your book. You don't want to put a price point on a barcode until you know how many pages your book will be. Most times, that estimate is indefinite until the editor brushes up the final edits and the book is formatted for print. Once this has been completed, you will be able to measure your page count alongside other books similar to yours and choose how much you want to sell your book for. If you're planning to sell solely online, platforms like Amazon and Barnes & Noble will present a price range you should consider pricing your book for.

Step Eight: Register for Copyright

Arguably the most important aspect of the self-publishing process, registering for your copyright is the immediate step you should take next. You must register for your copyright as soon as the editor finishes the last stroke of her pen. It is in this step that you protect your work. Visit www.copyright.gov to begin registering for copyright. The fee is only $35 if you are the only author of your work. The price rises as you include co-authors or illustrators. Keep in mind that the journey to getting your official registered seal could be anywhere from six to nine months.

Don't wait to file for copyright registration. Do it as soon as the edits are complete. I made the mistake of waiting to register and by the time I got around to it, someone had already copy and pasted my entire book on an eBook hosting website for FREE and I couldn't even dispute it because I hadn't handled my business by applying for copyright. If you don't do anything else, DON'T hesitate protecting your book.

Step Nine: Identify a Printing Company (Local, Online, or Overseas) and Order First Print Run

Printing is up next! This is the step where you want to be intensely careful. Your caution during this step can and will save you a lot of money if you make sure to read thoroughly and answer questions slowly. Make sure you have a full understanding of all the fine print before you print your book with any company; especially online companies. The reason for this is because (when dealing with online companies) the likelihood of something being messed up could hold your process up a little longer than a local print company could.

Going Local

It can be a love/hate type situation going to a local printer to get your books printed. Of course, if you already have an established relationship with a print company in your area then you may just be in for a treat. However, if you're just making those local connections for the sake of printing this book, you want to make sure that this option is the right one for you.

The pros of using a local printer is that you can be a little more hands on if you're able to visit the facility and see the project through, you may also be able to get your books sooner than you would if you were purchasing from a company not in your area. Additionally, it may be easier to get the local company on the phone to work through any kinks that may arise with much more ease than non-local printers. You also don't have to pay for shipping, which is a win!

The cons, may not be cons to you but I will point out the few I've found. Since this local company could be a smaller business, there is a strong likelihood that the price to print your books is higher than what it could be if you were purchasing from a major printing company. Often times I've seen that local printers charge double and almost triple of what Createspace would charge for the same book.

Uploading to Createspace & Kindle

Createspace is Amazon's partner company that helps independent authors become published authors by offering print-on-demand services and book hosting. Print-On-Demand differs from other print styles wherein if you choose this option, you are able to print as little to as many books as you would like at a time. This means that Createspace will allow you to purchase one, five, one hundred twenty-five, or one thousand two hundred and fifty books if you'd like. There is no limit or minimum to print-on-demand companies which comes in handy when you don't have all the funds you need to purchase a large amount of books in bulk from those other guys.

Createspace is an easy to use platform where they will literally walk you through the step-by-step process of answering all the questions you need and uploading all the necessary documents to execute the printing mission. You are able to price your book, set up your account for your royalties, and even convert your paperback option over to the eBook option using Amazon's Kindle.

When you upload your book to Createspace for printing, you automatically are granted the option to set up your Kindle account and convert that manuscript to eBook format. You do not have to have one option to get the other either. In fact, I actually published my first book using the Kindle eBook format and sold my book that way until I was able to earn enough money to actually have them printed. Although, my first official print run was with a local book printing company, I've seen firsthand what publishing with Createspace has done for my clients and my books thereafter. Kindle is no exception. The platform is easily the most used eBook reading go-to and its one of my personal favorites to read all of my favorite authors' work. I highly recommend using the Kindle option for eBooks, even if you don't print with Createspace.

Other Online Platforms

The same methods you would use to upload your book to Createspace and Kindle can be used for Barnes & Noble, Nook, SelfPublishing.Com, and even iBooks. You simply need to follow the step by step questions, upload the necessary documents, and set your price points. Though, with iBooks you will need access to a MacBook computer to upload your book to their platform. Keep in mind that there are differences in these companies, so be sure to read the fine print; especially when it discusses your royalties (the amount of money you will receive per every book sold).

Lastly, I offer Self-Publishing Coaching. If you are not looking to Partner Publish with me, that is okay. You can still receive a crash course from me where I will walk you through each step to make sure you have a successful self-publishing experience. You can email me at editor@theliteraryrevolutionary.com to inquire more.

Read This:
When Your Book Is Finally In Your Hands

If you follow the blueprint and start marketing your book long before it comes out, then when it's finally in your hand you won't have to work as hard initially. You should take this time to have an official book launch. This launch can be a party, a book signing, or even an online celebration. The goal now is to sell books to not only make back the money you invested in the project, but to also begin to make a nice profit from your literary contribution. Listed below are a few ways I prepare to market my book before, during, and after its launch. This section will only provide the key tips, as I will be penning a second title to this series that will go more in depth of what it means to be an Authorpreneur.

<u>Book Launch Marketing</u>

- o   Write and send a press release to local media outlets to attend your book launch

- Write and send press release to local and national media outlets to offer interviews
- LIVESTREAM your Book Launch (This could be considered a simultaneous Virtual Book Launch)
- Offer a sale at your book launch. Examples: 2 for 1, Buy 2 Get 1 Free, Bundles, etc.

EBook Marketing

- Once book is set up with Amazon Kindle, you can opt for Amazon to market your book for a small fee.
- Request your book to be selected for Kindle Unlimited (this will not get you as many sales, but it will get you visibility and hopefully reviews)

Grassroots Marketing

- Register for vending opportunities to have your book sold at events.
- Contact local small business owned bookstores and see what the requirements are to have your books sold in their store.

- Seek out non-traditional businesses to sell your books in (Hair Salons, Doctor's Offices, Gyms, etc.) Whatever your book discusses, find a relatable location to pitch to.
- Become a vendor for local colleges and universities and seek to have your book sold in school bookstores.
- Register your book with the Library of Congress, donate it to a few libraries in the area, or request that libraries purchase your books for the facility.
- Make sure to have business cards, bookmarks, and banners created and available for in- person connections and vending opportunities.
- Pitch to distribution companies to get your books in markets across the country and world.

Bonus: Tips for Your Genre

Nonfiction Tips

People connect with people and not things. They also have a difficult time connecting with concepts and theories when they are unsure of the origin of the theory. Simply put, we don't believe everything we see or read, and we only believe half of what we hear. When you're writing a nonfiction book, you should make sure you implement the 3 T's.

Your nonfiction book should tell your story (or a story) because transparency creates trust and your reader wants to be able to trust that you know your stuff. If you are aiming to target a specific group of people to share your knowledge with, offering your story will help you find that audience. It will help you to better serve the people who need you. It will weed out the people who have no real interest in what you have to offer and make room for those who do.

Your nonfiction book should show what you know. You want to be able to teach something throughout the pages of a nonfiction text. It literally should bleed your expertise or knowledge in a particular subject and solidify you as an authority in the topic at hand. Your readers will want to know how it is that you know what you're talking about. This is your opportunity to deliver.

Lastly, your nonfiction book should tell the reader how you can help or what can help them. The reader needs a takeaway from the text. Without the takeaway, their reading will have been in vain. You want to explain how things work, and why things are the way that they are. How can your reader feel empowered when reading your book? That's a question you have to ask yourself when you're following the 3 T's.

Your Nonfiction Book Should Do The Following:
1) <u>Tell</u> Your Story
2) <u>Teach</u> What You Know
3) Leave Your Reader with a <u>Takeaway</u>

Fiction Tips

Create characters your readers will fall in love with.

I was speaking at a conference in New York not too long ago, and someone from the audience asked me, "How do you fall in love with your characters?" I thought her question was significant because it's so important that we fall in love with our characters when writing fiction. If we don't, who will?

So I posed this question: How do you fall in love with real people? Is it by the way they dress? The way they speak to you? The things they do for the world? For you? How good you feel around them? How close you are? How much they make you feel loved? The same attributes that make you fall in love with the people in your life whether it be family, friends, your children, spouse or significant other can be used to make your readers fall in love with the characters and ultimately the storyline of your books. Sure, there will be some characters whose role is not ideal, yet the time and energy you invest in describing their unappealing presence in your story should reflect the level of care you put into shaping your characters. Period.

I tend to have the keen sense of using bits and pieces of character traits from people I know and love to create the ideal characters for my stories. For example in my upcoming Fiction Novel, *For the Love of Us*, I take several traits from my first love/boyfriend to help me construct the smoothest, cockiest, bossiest (if that's a word) "Souljah" I possibly can. Because my "real life" Souljah made me fall in love with him, I want my readers to fall in love with him just like I did. I want the sisters who read this book to desire a "Souljah" in their lives, and for the brothers to want to be like a "Souljah". The best way for your readers to love the characters you create is for you to love them and love on them throughout the entire writing process.

The Recipe:

Infinite Care + Immaculate Description = Character Love

<u>Make it memorable.</u>

Back in the day, my best friend Khaja and I used to be members of this blog styled online forum community called "All-star Fan Fiction" where young girls like she and I would create totally fiction stories about our favorite celebrities, and then publish them on the message board for people to read, comment, and review. As a matter of fact, Khaja, was one of the most well-known fan-fiction writers during that time and she dominated many stories related to the members of the singing groups B5 and B2K.

Go ahead and laugh.

Yes, we were those girls. But that's beside the point.

There was one particular story that I remember so vividly because of a particular scene that took place in it, and I'm reminded of that story every single time I hear a certain song. In this fan fiction piece, singer (J-Boog from B2K) had been in a complicated relationship with his girl for some time. They had been fighting their love for one another during the entire story, and in the final scene they were forced to dance together at a party when they realized everyone else was booed up and they were the only two without a partner. That dance led into the long awaited "happily ever after" ending; marriage, children, house, family, success, etc. But, what made this scene stick out so much to the point that even ten years later today I remember it so vividly is the song they danced to. The music playing at the dance was Joe - *I Wanna Know*. So here it is, every time I hear I Wanna Know, I think back to that story and I wish for the life of me that I could locate it on the web somewhere so I can reread it for the umpteenth time. It was my absolute favorite fan fiction story of all time - extremely well written, characters fully developed, setting A-1, and plot thickening by the minute. If anyone knows the sister that wrote that piece, holla at me! I want to publish it. ;)

But, seriously...

As a writer, I've always wanted to have that type of effect on my readers - and you should too. When writing fiction, try adding in some creative non-fiction to the text. You want your audience to have a lasting remembrance of your work. They should recall bits and pieces of your book from the little things they may encounter in their real lives. In this case, the usage of a popular song *"I Wanna Know"* playing in the background during one of the longest anticipated scenes in the story marinated in my memory so well that now there's never a time I don't think about the story when I hear Joe in my ears. It literally will forever live in my memory.

Though there are several ways to write a memorable fiction story, five of the easiest ways is by simply incorporating the five senses: sight, smell, sound, taste and touch. Using the five senses to create a memorable fiction story is not a hidden secret and it could honestly be the thing that makes your story what it is. Don't shy away from being as descriptive as possible when writing fiction, either. Description is what turns an ordinary fiction story into an extraordinary piece of literature.

Tips for Memoirs/Autobiographies

Say you're writing a book about a particular event or time in your life. If you find that you are writing in narrative form, you are essentially writing a memoir. Now, there's a difference between a memoir and an autobiography. Your memoir is an account of a particular time period or event that took place in your life. You could write about your childhood from ages 6-18 and how it affected a part of your life as an adult. You could write about your children and what life has been or was like raising them. You could write about your journey to becoming who you are as a career-driven and business minded woman, and maybe even talk about some of the funny or heart-wrenching stories that have come with the journey. The truth is, you can write as many memoirs as you want because as mentioned before, memoirs take on a specific moment in time or event that took place.

An autobiography on the other hand is a bit more in depth and complex. When you decide on writing an autobiography, you are essentially spilling out your guts on your entire life up until this point. Most times, autobiographies are reserved for people who are up in age, who have lived a long life and are unsure when the final days are coming. This isn't always the case for autobiographical pieces, but oftentimes it is. Another demographic that may consider writing an autobiography may be public or political figures of some sort. Consider the leaders of the Civil Rights Movement and the Black Panther Party. Quite a few of the prominent names we know (both deceased and alive) are still talked about to this day because they wrote their life stories out for us to know in detail who they were, where they came from, why they thought they were important, and what the world may have thought of them. These leaders turned authors have not all waited until they were up in age to write their story, for most times there was uncertainty in whether they would live long enough to tell their story later.

  Two very significant women that stand out to me most when I think of leaders who took the initiative to document their stories before their time was up is Ida B. Wells-Barnett and Assata Shakur. Ida was a prolific journalist, newspaper editor, suffragist, and one of the early leaders of the Civil Rights Movement. She was the voice of the Anti-Lynching Campaign and she began documenting her autobiography well before her passing. She got it so far up to speed that it only took her daughter to finish off the last of it, have it edited and ready for print shortly after.

Assata Shakur is widely known as a key former member of the Black Liberation Army and Black Panther Party. Assata was accused of killing a New Jersey Interstate Trooper along with Baba Zayd Malik (RIP) and Baba Sundiata Acoli who is still in prison to this day. Assata was liberated from her incarceration by members of an "elite squad" as I like to call them, and she is now living in Cuba. However, I am sure that Assata did not know if she would ever be able to live in asylum where the United States could not come for her again, which is why I'm sure she put out *Assata An Autobiography*, well before she got up in age. She understood that her story was profound, that many people wanted to know the truth about what happened the night she was arrested and charged with murder, and that many young activists, organizers and warriors alike could benefit from knowing her story to be more careful and aware of the circumstances and scrutiny enemies of the state face.

Things you want to do when writing YOUR story:
1) Use your five senses to help you recall memories.
2) Create a playlist of the songs/shows/events that take you back; put you in the mind frame of reliving some things.
3) Write down every emotion that comes to mind when you reflect in time. Expound on each.

Tips for Children's Books

Though I have not personally published any children's books of my own as of yet, I am looking forward to the day that not only me, but my son begins to write and publish for children. It's definitely a goal of mine and I believe that once I do get to that point where there are published Children's titles to my name, I'll have much more to share about the journey. In the meantime, I just want to touch on the few tips Award Winning Children's Book Author & Publisher Akua Agusi of (www.cultivatedrootsmedia.com) shared while on my Literary Black Girl Magic Series back in 2017:

1) Test your book idea out on children. One thing you can depend on is a child to tell you the honest truth.
2) Make sure the content is age appropriate to the age level you assign it for. Setting an age level for a book that hasn't been tested on children of that age level is essentially false promoting. Be sure.
3) Include teaching moments. Every opportunity with children is an opportunity to teach them something. This is no different when writing a book.

BONUS CHAPTER:
Does Your Brand Need A Book?

Recently, I realized my brand needed a book and this book you are reading is a product of that realization. The theme of my first ever LIVE 3-Part Teaching Series I hosted on Instagram was called, "How to Secure the Bag as an Author in 2018". By December of 2017, I had conducted a serious purge in my email list and Facebook Group because it seemed that somewhere and somehow, the spark was lost with my audience. I wasn't quite sure what had gone wrong. I wondered if it was me. Maybe I wasn't as consistent as I should have been when folks first joined my tribe, or maybe my audience was no longer interested in writing books? I couldn't quite tell, and before I thought to ask my audience, I ended up deleting everybody who did not adhere to requirements to stay down.

Once the purge was completed, I focused all of my new and revitalized energy into pouring into the folks who chose to stay. I began marketing my ass off to bring in new faces in my space. I was very clear this time around about who I wanted to assist, whereas, in the beginning of the year I was just marketing to anybody and their mama who wanted to write a book. It became clear to me that the audience which would benefit the most from my experience, and would also be willing to pay for my expertise and assistance were working women between the ages of 26-48. Many of the women in this newfound tribe were entrepreneurs, brand influencers, teachers, women in business, public figures and even politicians. This was the market I had secretly always wanted to reach, seeing as though when I screened my history of clients, I identified that my most ideal client fit in this demographic.

    Being very clear on who my services and products were for led me into crafting a powerful LIVE Series and in turn spawned the idea for this book. I realized that my tweets of encouragement, motivation, and tips for successful writing stuck well with many women of this demographic. If you follow me on Twitter or on Instagram then you know I stamp most if not all of my tweets and postings with the #WriteTheBookSis. After noticing that those particular posts got the most engagement, I decided to put all of it in a book. See how that works?

    I give this story background because I want you to take inventory of the messages, posts, and tweets you may put out for your brand and/or business. You have an opportunity here to do the same thing that I did to figure out what resonates with your audience so well that it should be in a book. Don't get intimidated by the usage of the term "brand" if you don't have a business of your own. Your brand is you. Essentially, it is the image you portray to the world and it is how people remember who you are and what you offer and are capable of. You are a walking, talking, breathing billboard and you stand for something. The people that know you can help you identify your brand's message (what your life and the way you carry yourself says about you), or you can identify what that is based on what you know people gravitate to the most about you. You can also be a vessel for several brands, as I am.

    For example: My very first "brand" was that of a singer/vocalist. Before I began writing books, serving in the social justice arena, running my own businesses, or even becoming a dope mama, I was "The Voice". Growing up, that was what I was known for because I was often put on the spot to sing and bring healing by way of my vocal chords to people who were hurting. Whether I was leading the church choir with my solos on Sunday morning, singing lullabies to the babies in the nursery at school, putting on a sidewalk show for the homeless and less fortunate downtown, opening up the Atlanta Hawks game, or offering the strongest of bellows on the bullhorn at a rally or march – I was that girl who could sing the roof off of the place and create chills down folks' spine. No matter where I go in my city, even to this day and after all of the other things I've accomplished or been acknowledged for taking on, my initial brand is "Nia, the girl who sings for the people".

    The great part about deciding on a book for your brand is that you get to choose which brand of yours you want to write a book for. You can decide this by identifying which brand's audience will benefit most from your words in a book, which brand book will be most profitable, or which brand book can take you many places. Most times, the brand book you decide to write will do all three of these things for you, plus more. I knew that although "vocalist" was my initial brand and was the one most people knew about me, writing a book about it would not quite do much for me because it's not like my voice was going to sing out through the pages. In most cases dealing with the arts, it's a little more challenging to create published texts to exemplify your contribution to the artistic arena – unless of course you are a visual artist or even a poet.

    For me though, I knew that at the age of 21 (the beginning of my life as many elders would say), even if I thought I had a lot to say about my brand as "The Voice", I knew it wouldn't be received by that many people because at 21 they would say I haven't even lived long enough to have a story to tell. Although, I don't believe that to be true (because we all have stories to tell) I knew that once I did decide to write about being "The Voice", I wanted it to be in my autobiography much later down the line. So, I went with the next and most needed brand book at the time, *"Young Black Fearless: The 7 Step Guide to Activism"*. Luckily enough, I was able to weave in being "The Voice" of the Atlanta movement during the time of the heightened rallies and marches protesting police terrorism.

Young Black Fearless was my debut book and provided that level of respect and acknowledgement that I desired for not only myself, but other young women activists in the movement. I saw where there was a great disparity in the level of recognition that the men received for their efforts than with women, and oftentimes this felt like a slap in the face to me because I knew of how much work and effort went into the grassroots organizing efforts of these actions. Women led the charge, mainly. I knew that I did not want to be just another black woman who would spend her entire life working on behalf of the people, only to be completely disregarded and not acknowledged for the hard work and effort I put in. I had heard too many horror stories of this in the past, and having read a ton of memoirs and autobiographies of courageous historical black women who dealt with the same things, I knew I did not want that to be my story. Now, this is not to say that it doesn't still happen most times, and it's not to shade any other women who have not written books yet – but this is just a testament that my documentation of my experiences as a grassroots organizer forced some folks to put some respect on my name.

I also know for a fact that had I not documented, published, and marketed my book in such a way that branded me as an authority on the topic, I would not be asked to sit on panel discussions to answer questions and offer analyses or advice, nor would I be traveling to speak at colleges and universities around the country. My book was my ticket; my tool to level up and gain respect as more than just an overworked and burnt out activist. Thankfully it also created a lucrative stream of side income, which never hurt anybody.

Knowing When Your Brand Needs a Book

There are four main ways to know your brand needs a book:

1) If you provide a service that helps people do something or become someone.
2) If you offer a product that is not exactly self-explanatory and would benefit from a little more information about how to use it, what it's for, and what you can do with it.

3) You are a public figure of some sort and you have a story to tell that will lead more people to your flock and help you walk through some doors you may be struggling to get through currently.
4) You have knowledge of a particular topic and are proficient in it enough to help others understand it. You understand that you can use this as a tool to gain credibility for your expertise in a given subject.

There are several things a book can do for your brand, but here are a few:

Writing a book can serve as a marketing tool for your brand.

As entrepreneurs, influencers, and public figures, we are always looking for ways that we can market ourselves in the sometimes overly saturated industries. Often, these marketing techniques can seem so routine that it can be challenging to stand out from others in the industry doing the same thing you do. One of the ways to direct more attention your way is to write a really good book. Whether you write a book about what you can offer people, or how to do something industry related, creating a piece of literature that can travel places faster than you can sometimes will help potential clients and customers find you. Word of mouth travels extremely fast, and someone may have heard of your book before ever knowing that you or your business/brand existed. The introduction to your book will then help them get acquainted with who you are which begins to build that trust needed to spend money with you.

What I've learned through my role in community and even in my business is that a lot of the questions that people ask on a regular basis regarding your area of expertise can most times be answered through the pages of your book. Halfway into my journey as a full-time entrepreneur, I learned to turn on my sound recorder when I spoke to clients and they asked me questions because I quickly realized that I would be repeating the same answers to questions each time a new person asked. I decided to use those client check-ins as opportunities to write pages to this exact book. Many of the topics and pointers I offer you come from the many questions clients and potential clients have asked to help them write their books.

I could have easily created a list of questions and answers to post to my website, but then they wouldn't include personal experiences, explanations, and testimonies in a fashion that would help you to connect. Furthermore, as a business woman, what profit would I attain from giving away all of my good content with no plan to monetize from it? Hence, this book was birthed.

In this day and age, with net neutrality being a threat to American society and the future of our access to affordable internet, now is the time to document and publish all the content you've acquired for your brand, for the sake of its longevity. Books are slowly but surely taking the places of business cards. When you really think about it, how often do you hold on to business cards longer than a few days before you can't find it anymore? Exactly! When was the last time you accidently threw a book away? If ever?

<u>Writing a book raises your brand's visibility and exposure, and it helps to establish your credibility in the subject matter to where people will respect you as an authority in the field.</u>

If pitched properly, you book could land media features beyond what you believe! Trust me, I hadn't imagined any of the features I've been granted the opportunity to have before becoming an author. The great thing about media attention is that a few more people now know your name and what you do. This is one of the ultimate goals for brands and business. We want people to know our names and what we do so that people will keep us in mind and will spend their money on us. Attention turns into money and opportunities for expansion. Without the attention of outlets shining light on your work and efforts, you can miss out on a whole consumer base that would be ready and willing to purchase from you, book you, or become a client from you if only they knew you existed. If there is nothing I love helping my clients do more, it is helping them use their book as a tool to establish credibility and make additional coins.

Client Spotlights

I had a client who had been working on a program for years! She put in a lot of work in the name of her organization, but it wasn't until she realized her book that people started to recognize her as the expert in the field and media stayed knocking on her door. Her book helped to highlight her work in such a way that she's gained opportunities to teach her program nationally and internationally. She's gearing up to be the keynote speaker for a conference in South Africa very soon because of her work as an author!

Client Spotlight

Another client of mine went from being just another barber with a booth at the Bronner Brother's show to becoming a returning judge for the hair show due to his expertise reflected in his book, *The Cutting Edge* and the media attention he received from the book.

Writing a book helps potential customers/clients connect with you on a personal level.

I've had people not want to use my services because they felt they were already looked at as credible. One lady I met at a conference even said to me, "What do I need to write a book for when people can just google me?" Though googling you may be a quick way to establish your credibility in a sense, you have to remember that the articles written by other people about you are just that. Articles written by OTHER people about YOU. Journalists and bloggers are not capable of showing off what you know better than you, and while you may think what you know can easily be searched on the site, the reality of it is – some people just don't want to read articles alone. They want to get deeper into the content. They want to know the story of the face behind the content. Writing a book helps leads connect with you to the point where even if you say a little, they think they know a lot. When people think they know you, or somehow feel connected to you, they are more likely to purchase from you or hire you.

<u>Client Spotlight</u>

One of my former clients, a hairstylist, has had tremendous success with her book because of how raw and uncut her story is. She did not hold back from telling her truth of being a teen mother turned entrepreneur who struggled with her identity, as she learned early in life that her parents were not who she knew them to be. However, the edge she provided accompanied with her personality which drove people to purchase her book made her a bestselling author within a month of publishing!

<u>Client Spotlight</u>

One of my most recent clients basically sold out of pre-orders of her book. She offered her story of losing her mother and instantly attracted others who'd lost mothers. These were her key customers (and those who purchased for loved ones grieving). She established herself as an authority in therapy, specializing in grief.

However, because she used her story as the basis, she connected with those who hadn't considered seeing a therapist but now could relate to one. She had a speaking engagement the very next day after her book launch party and has had quite a few book customers turn into clients since.

About the Author

Nia Sadé Akinyemi, best known as, "*The Literary Revolutionary*" teaches women how to revolutionize their brands by writing, publishing, and marketing powerful books with ease and confidence. She helps her clients flip their manuscripts into literary masterpieces through her signature author coaching, editing, and partner publishing services. People come to Nia when they have a story to tell, knowledge to share, or expertise to offer and they want to put it all in a book and she prides herself in helping her clients gain respect as authorities in their lives and in their fields through published texts.

Nia is a literary activist and influencer who stresses the importance of writing stories, documenting history, and cataloging knowledge. She is the mother to her handsome son, Israel, and she enjoys writing while burning candles from her Hand poured 100% All Natural Soy Candle Company, Scent Messages. www.discoverscentmessages.com

For Booking

To book Nia Sadé Akinyemi to speak at your event, sit on a panel discussion, feature as a guest on your platform, or to facilitate a writing workshop for your event or organization, email:

invite@theliteraryrevolutionary.com

Join the A-Team

To join my exclusive coaching group, "Nia's A-Team" to receive monthly access to all of my Masterclasses, Trainings, EBooks, Workbooks, and Discounts on all of my services for only $17/mo. Visit: www.theliteraryrevolutionary.com/a-team

Follow Nia

To follow me on all social media, visit the links below.

www.instagram.com/niasadeakinyemi

www.facebook.com/theliteraryrevolutionary

www.twitter.com/niasadeakinyemi

www.periscope.tv/niasadeakinyemi

Join Mailing List

To join my mailing list, visit:

www.theliteraryrevolutionary.com/write

Services

To learn more about my author coaching, editing, and partner publishing services and current rates, visit:

www.theliteraryrevolutionary.com/services

Black Authors Matter

To learn more about the Black Authors Matter campaign, visit:

www.blackauthorsmatter.com

Scent Messages LLC

To purchase a writing candle or ANY candle from my All Natural Soy Candle Company as a gift, décor, or simply for your own use visit: www.discoverscentmessages.com

New titles are coming soon!!

www.ingramcontent.com/pod-product-compliance
Lightning Source LLC
Chambersburg PA
CBHW060135100426
42744CB00007B/792